QuickBooks 2025 Handbook

The Comprehensive Guide to Easily Managing Your Finances, Mastering Bookkeeping, and Advancing Your Business

Tim Elvis

QB quickbooks 2025

CHAPTER ONE
A BRIEF OVERVIEW OF QUICKBOOKS 2025

QuickBooks: What is it?

One of the most widely used accounting programs for small companies is QuickBooks. If you're searching for a better option than what you're presently using, QuickBooks may be a terrific, affordable alternative to spreadsheets, manual accounting, or other software.

QuickBooks offers small companies a broad range of accounting and financial services, despite its reputation as a bookkeeping tool. Here are a few examples:

- **QuickBooks Payroll:** Businesses may use this program to pay up to fifty workers at once by check or direct deposit. Both full-service and self-service options are offered. If you choose a full-service plan, your W-2 forms for local, state, and federal taxes are automatically calculated and mailed at the end of the year.
- **QuickBooks Commerce:** This consolidated dashboard shows real-time inventory and order progress information. With QuickBooks Commerce's scalability, you can quickly add more sales channels, build your B2B commerce platform, and connect to internet marketplaces.
- **QuickBooks Online:** This cloud-based accounting program lets you access and see your records at any time and from any device. This service may also be used to create invoices.
- **QuickBooks Live:** With QuickBooks Live, you can now hire a qualified bookkeeper to help you with all of your accounting needs.
- **QuickBooks Payments:** This feature allows you to generate pay-enabled invoices, set up recurring invoices, and accept digital payments while you're on the go. Your customers have the option to pay digitally.
- **QuickBooks Time:** Use QuickBooks Time to monitor billable hours for clients, payroll, or projects. It's easy to keep track of hours and payments using QuickBooks Payroll.

Together with QuickBooks accounting software, these apps may help you set up a comprehensive accounting and payments environment for your small or medium-sized company.

The Operation of QuickBooks

You don't have to sign up for every QuickBooks service; you may choose which ones to utilize. You may always add new apps as your requirements change, but apps like payroll or accounting software are excellent starting points. As you need services, you may upgrade or remove them. The first step in a typical setup is to register for QuickBooks. QuickBooks Live may then be added to further customize your system to meet your requirements. As your business grows, you'll need full-time employees, contractors, and freelancers. Following that, you can use QuickBooks Time to begin monitoring billable hours and QuickBooks Payroll to streamline monthly payments.

Options for QuickBooks Software

- **The Invoicing:** Many businesses see invoicing as a crucial responsibility, especially those in the service sector or those that rely on independent contractors. QuickBooks makes it simple to create invoices, regardless of whether you're beginning from scratch or using an estimate you've already created. It is even possible to establish invoices for recurring payments. The invoice must then be sent to the client or printed out and delivered to them in physical form. Reports such as the total amount owed to customers, the number of unpaid bills, and the specifics of each invoice—whether paid or past due—can be easily performed and examined.

- **Monitoring Bills and Expenses:** Linking your bank and credit card accounts will be an option when you set up QuickBooks. After then, QuickBooks will monitor every transaction you make without your involvement. Even if bill tracking is automated, it is still possible to conduct it by hand. Manually documenting a transaction is simple, regardless of whether you're working with cash or checks. In summary, QuickBooks provides a wide range of reports that may assist you in reviewing your financial expenditures. If you have a list of invoices on hand, you may easily monitor upcoming payments and make timely payments.

- **Monitoring Employee Time and Expenses:** QuickBooks makes it simple to track the time and billable expenses that employees or independent contractors spend. They may choose to have a bookkeeper input the data for them or use the QuickBooks mobile app to do it themselves.

- **Internet-Based Payments:** As a company owner, you understand the importance of keeping a steady flow of revenue. QuickBooks Payments makes it simple to accept online payments when you issue invoices from inside QuickBooks. If your company has many locations throughout the globe, QuickBooks allows you to accept payments in local currencies. Before deciding to use QuickBooks, it is wise to confirm that software is compatible with the currency you deal in. Every transaction is recorded as soon as it occurs.

- **Payroll:** Processing payroll is essential for every business. You may choose how often payroll is computed automatically with the payroll add-on. As your company expands, you have three choices for adding functionality. Small and medium-sized companies may add services like same-day direct deposit and expert setup help to the Core plan, which provides everything they need to get started.

The Advantages of QuickBooks for Your Company

Enrolling in QuickBooks, one of the most popular accounting software packages, greatly increases the likelihood that other platforms your business utilizes, such as CRM, will be able to communicate with it and streamline processes. QuickBooks is now offering two promotions: a free 30-day trial and a 50% discount for the first three months after enrollment. Here are just a few of the many ways QuickBooks might benefit your business.

Easy Accessibility to Financial Statements

You have easy access to all of the usual financial papers, such as the income statement, balance sheet, statement of cash flows, and tax returns. You may choose to print these statements and provide them to your accountant at the time of filing, or you can ask them to see them without a login ID and password.

Simple Inventory Control

It may be quite difficult to keep track of inventory as it sells, input the information into the appropriate expense account, and calculate taxable revenue at the end of the fiscal year. QuickBooks makes it simple because of how much it automates. Every time you get payment for an item in inventory, your taxable revenue is instantly changed and the relevant expenditure account is updated.

Simple Taxation

Tax season may be challenging and stressful for a number of reasons. QuickBooks streamlines your business's financial operations by automatically calculating revenue and expenses as they arise. The automatic tax computation every cycle does not exclude payroll, which has a high tax burden. Everything your accountant needs to finish the taxes should be printed out and sent to them in a single, handy package. If you use the QuickBooks mobile app to scan and upload your receipts immediately, you won't have to rush to collect them when tax time arrives. If you would like, you can also invite them to see the reports and download any necessary files.

2025 QuickBooks: What's New?

Automatic Feeds from Banks

- **Automatic Import and classification:** Compared to manual data input, automated import and classification of bank transactions saves a significant amount of time.

Improved Bank Reconciliation

- **Better Tools:** The updated tools make it simple and accurate to reconcile your bank statements with your QuickBooks data.

Advanced Pricing and Reporting

- **Detailed Financial Reports:** To learn more about your company, create thorough financial reports.
- **Complex Pricing Management:** Easily handle intricate pricing plans.

Management of Integrated Inventory

- **Inventory tracking:** Easily manage orders and keep an eye on stock.
- **Supply Chain Operations:** Standardize your supply chain processes to save time and effort.

Costing a Job

- **Project Monitoring:** You may monitor project costs and profitability with the help of comprehensive tools.

Integrated Payroll

Simplified Payroll Processing: Using QuickBooks to handle payroll processing makes it easier to manage employee payments.

Tracking Time

Employee Hours Management: Use QuickBooks to track and manage timesheets.

Tracking 1099

Contractor Management: Easily arrange and keep an eye on your contractors' 1099 documentation.

Easy Preparation of Taxes

Easy shift: A seamless shift from accounting to tax preparation may be achieved by ensuring that all the necessary data is available beforehand.

For whom is QuickBooks 2025 appropriate?

- **Owners of small businesses:** Perhaps small company owners are the main target demographic for QuickBooks 2025. The software's full financial management features include handling payroll, generating invoices, keeping track of income and expenses, and preparing for tax season. QuickBooks allows small company owners to focus on growing their operations by simplifying and streamlining accounting procedures.

- **Independent Contractors and Freelancers:** Numerous freelancers and independent contractors have particular financial needs; include tracking multiple revenue streams, setting aside money for certain tasks, and determining how to claim tax deductions. With the help of QuickBooks 2025's features like mileage monitoring, cost tracking, and invoicing, freelancers can stay organized and ensure they are accurately reporting their earnings.

- **Businesses of a Medium Size:** The accounting needs of expanding companies are becoming more complex. QuickBooks 2025 is an excellent choice for medium-sized enterprises because to its features, which include financial forecasting, budgeting, and inventory management. The software's robust reporting functions, which provide insights into financial performance, may help businesses make better strategic decisions.

- **Nonprofit Establishments:** Nonprofits may utilize QuickBooks 2025's customized features for fund accounting, grants, and donations. This software helps nonprofits meet their legal requirements while demonstrating financial transparency to donors and stakeholders.

- **New Businesses:** Startups need a reliable accounting system to monitor their finances from the beginning. QuickBooks 2025's budgeting, cash flow management, and expenditure tracking tools are essential for businesses with little funding. Because this program is so user-friendly, company founders don't need much training to use it.

- **Shopkeepers:** Retail businesses need to be able to track sales and handle inventories accurately. QuickBooks 2025 has features for managing stocks, creating sales reports, and integrating with point-of-sale systems. Stores may improve their operational efficiency and financial management using these tools.

- **Companies That Provide Services:** QuickBooks 2025's time tracking and invoicing features are perfect for service-based businesses like consultants, repair services, and marketing agencies. The tool makes it feasible to accurately charge based on hours worked or services rendered, which enhances cash flow and customer satisfaction.
- **Qualified Bookkeepers and Accountants:** The preferred program for qualified accountants and bookkeepers, QuickBooks 2025, may help you better manages your clients' finances. The software's multi-user capability allows accountants to collaborate with their customers in real-time. QuickBooks' sophisticated reporting features enable accountants to provide their clients with incisive analysis and wise financial guidance.
- **Property managers and real estate brokers:** Property managers and real estate agents may utilize QuickBooks 2025 to monitor rental income, expenses, and financial reports for the properties under their supervision. Maintaining accurate records and fulfilling all relevant tax responsibilities is made simpler by using this tool, which streamlines the accounting procedures involved in property management.
- **Producers:** Manufacturers need strong inventory management and cost monitoring solutions for efficient production process management. The tracking tools in QuickBooks 2025 let you to monitor your inventory of finished goods, work-in-progress, and raw materials. Manufacturers may also benefit from the software's task-costing and financial reporting features.
- **Experts in Health and Wellbeing:** If you work in the health and wellness sector as a physician, therapist, or personal trainer, QuickBooks 2025 may be used to manage the financial aspects of your business. Since the software helps with patient payment monitoring, spending management, and financial report production, healthcare professionals can focus on giving patients high-quality care.
- **Farming Enterprises:** There are specific accounting needs for agricultural businesses, including tracking crop and animal expenses, managing farm income, and anticipating seasonal fluctuations. QuickBooks 2025 provides solutions to address these areas and assist farmers and agricultural businesses in maintaining accurate financial records.
- **Online Retailers:** Among the most crucial elements of managing an online company are sales, inventory, and shipping expenses. Thanks to QuickBooks 2025's connectivity with several e-commerce platforms, businesses can now manage their sales data and finances in one convenient location. This link may

help online businesses streamline their operations and improve the accuracy of their financial records.

+ **Educational Establishments:** QuickBooks 2025 may be used by colleges and universities for grant and donation processing, tuition monitoring, and financial administration. The program's reporting capabilities may be used by educational institutions to maintain transparency and accountability in their budgets.

+ **Home-Based Enterprises:** Even though they can be smaller, home-based businesses nevertheless need trustworthy accounting services. Because it offers affordable alternatives with essential functionality like financial reporting, invoicing, and cost management, QuickBooks 2025 is ideal for home-based businesses.

CHAPTER TWO
THE SYSTEM SPECIFICATIONS

System Software

- Windows 11, all editions including 64-bit, natively installed
- Windows 10, all editions including 64-bit, natively installed
- Windows 8.1 (Update 1), all editions including 64-bit, natively installed
- Windows Server 2022
- Windows Server 2019
- Windows Server 2016
- Windows Server 2012 R2, natively installed

The processor

- 2.4 GHz is the minimum
- RAM operating at 3.0 GHz or above is recommended.
- 4 GB is the minimum.
- Recommendation: 8 GB or more

The disk space

- 2.5 GB of storage space (data files demand more space).
- Extra software: the QuickBooks CD contains 60 MB of the Microsoft.NET 4.8 Runtime.

Screen resolution

- Designed for screens with a resolution of 1280 x 1024 or higher
- Ideally suited for 1920 x 1080 resolution or higher
- Accommodates up to two extended displays in addition to one workstation monitor.

Internet Access

- In order to use online services and payroll, a fast internet connection is necessary.

The optical drive

- Four DVD-ROM drives are needed to install CDs.

Compatibility of Software

- Microsoft Office:
  - ➢ Office 2016 on 32- and 64-bit systems, including Outlook 2016
  - ➢ Office 2013/365, which includes Outlook 2013, is available in 32- and 64-bit versions.
  - ➢ Office 2010 SP2, includes Outlook 2010 SP2, in both 32- and 64-bit versions
- **Email:** Outlook, Windows Mail, Gmail, and Yahoo Mail
- **Browsers:**
  - ➢ 32-bit Internet Explorer 11
  - ➢ Google Chrome
  - ➢ Microsoft Edge

Compatibility of Hardware

Supports the majority of common hardware accessories, including barcode readers, printers, and scanners.

Online System Requirements for QuickBooks 2025

Browsers and Operating Systems

- Windows 11
- Windows 10
- macOS 11 Big Sur or later
- Google Chrome: The latest version
- Firefox: Latest version
- Microsoft Edge: Latest version
- Safari 13 or later (Mac only)

Internet Access

- DSL, cable, or a faster internet connection is advised.

Extra requirements

- **Adobe Reader:** To print forms, the most recent version is needed.
- **PDF Viewer:** Required to read PDF files

Recommended setup for performance optimization

Recommended setup for desktop version

- Operating System: Windows 11 or Windows 10, 64-bit
- Processor: 3.0 GHz multi-core processor
- RAM: 16 GB
- Disk Space: SSD with at least 10 GB of free space
- Monitor: 1920 x 1080 resolution or higher, dual monitors

Recommended setup for online version

- Browser: Google Chrome or Microsoft Edge, latest versions
- Internet Connection: Fiber optic or high-speed cable connection
- Monitor: 1920 x 1080 resolution or higher

Setting up and installing

1. Get QuickBooks 2025.
- **Go to the page where QuickBooks may be downloaded:** Launch your web browser and go to the QuickBooks Downloads & Updates page on the official QuickBooks website.
- **Pick Your Own Version:** After selecting your country and the product you need, choose QuickBooks 2025.
- **Get the Installer here:** Click on "Download" in the menu. You should store the installation file to a prominent location on your computer, such the desktop or a download folder.
2. Installing QuickBooks 2025.
- **Launch the installer:** Double-clicking the installer file you downloaded will start the installation procedure.
- **Type in the product and license numbers:** Your license and product numbers will be requested throughout the installation process. These may be found in the email that verifies your purchase or, if it's a boxed edition, in the physical packing.

- **Adhere to the on-screen directions:** You will get comprehensive instructions from the installer. Whether you want an Express Install or a Custom Install will be up to you:
  - ➤ **Express Install:** This option installs QuickBooks using the default settings and is recommended for most people.
  - ➤ **Custom Install:** This allows you to install certain features and choose the installation location, making it ideal for experienced users with special needs.
3. **Configure QuickBooks 2025.**
- **Turn on QuickBooks:** After the installation is complete, open QuickBooks. You will need to input your license and product information again throughout the software activation procedure. Follow the on-screen directions to complete the activation process.
- **Establish or Access a Company File:** If you are beginning from scratch, you may create a new business file. Enter your company's details by following the setup procedure. If you're upgrading from a previous version of QuickBooks, make sure you save a duplicate of your data before opening your existing QuickBooks file in QuickBooks 2025.
- **Configure Preferences:** Customize QuickBooks' settings to make it work for your company:
  - ➤ **Chart of Accounts:** Make or import your chart of accounts to efficiently monitor your money.
  - ➤ **Tax Rates:** Use the Tax Rates section to set your sales tax rates and apply them to the appropriate goods.
  - ➤ **User Permissions:** Assign users and set up their rights in accordance with their roles within the organization.
4. **Import Data and Link Bank Accounts**
- **Connect bank accounts:** Select "Link Account" from the Banking option in QuickBooks. Follow the on-screen directions to connect your bank accounts. Because QuickBooks can automatically import and organize your bank transactions, you will save a ton of time.
- **Bring in Data:** If you have data files or are switching from another accounting system, you may use QuickBooks' import features to get your data into the program. This might contain information about previous transactions, goods, services, suppliers, clients, and other pertinent data.
5. **Examine the Tools and Features**
- **Examine the New Features:** Please take the time to get familiar with QuickBooks 2025 and all of its enhanced and new features:

- ➢ **Improved Reporting:** Use advanced reporting tools to have a better understanding of your financial data.
- ➢ **Integrated Inventory Management:** Use Integrated Inventory Management to manage orders, monitor inventory levels, and boost supply chain effectiveness.
- ➢ **Payroll Integration:** Set up and handle payroll from inside QuickBooks for efficient employee payment processing.
- ✦ **Utilize Support Materials: Utilize the many help options available in QuickBooks:**
  - ➢ **Tutorials:** You may get step-by-step instructions to assist you with a range of tasks and activities.
  - ➢ **Customer Support:** If you have any questions or concerns about customer service, contact QuickBooks support. They may be reached via email, live chat, or phone.
  - ➢ **Community Forums:** Join the QuickBooks community to interact with other users, share ideas, and get assistance.

CHAPTER THREE
ABOUT INTERFACE NAVIGATION

An overview of the dashboard in QuickBooks

QuickBooks has a dashboard that is integrated to provide you a clear and practical overview of your business's financial situation. When you have access to the key indications, you can confidently manage your company's finances, inventory, and strategy.

The dashboard displays key performance indicators (KPIs) that affect your business in a number of different ways. The balances of your accounts payable and receivable, your profit or loss for the previous month, and the dates of your upcoming bills are a few instances of these indicators. QuickBooks' built-in dashboard does more than simply display statistics. It may alert you to things like past-due invoices or incorrect bank transactions, to name just two instances. The dashboard's layout may be changed by you. QuickBooks allows you to see, measure, and report on key financial performance metrics, but all of the representations are read-only. As a result, you will not be able to modify the time ranges or filters.

Is there a dashboard function in QuickBooks Desktop?

The desktop version of QuickBooks lacks an integrated dashboard feature, in contrast to QuickBooks Online.

However, you may still be able to quickly evaluate your financial status using the following techniques:

- The QuickBooks desktop Home Page shows some basic information, such as recent transactions and upcoming due dates. You may also use the Home page's insights to keep an eye on the state of your business.
- Among the financial reports that may be produced via the Reports Center are the Balance Sheet, Profit and Loss Statement, and Accounts Receivable / Payable Aging Reports. You may run these reports and change the date ranges to get a fast snapshot of your financial status.

Is it possible to design a unique dashboard for your QuickBooks Online information?

Spreadsheets or BI tools may be used to create a bespoke dashboard using the data that was exported from QuickBooks Online. Create your dashboard using an appropriate solution, such as Looker Studio. It goes without saying that you need to import your QuickBooks data. Spreadsheets, BI tools, and data warehouses are just a few of the many programs that may be integrated with QuickBooks Online using Coupler.io. Another option is to purchase a pre-made dashboard template. In this way, you may have a working analytics dashboard that is prepared to receive your data. The second option may be accessed manually or automatically using the QuickBooks Online connection in the template.

Examples of custom QuickBooks dashboards for analytics and reporting

Check out the free QuickBooks dashboard designs with built-in connection offered by Coupler.io. To put it another way, adding data to the dashboard just requires connecting it to your QuickBooks Online account.

Dashboard for QuickBooks revenue

The revenue dashboard makes it easy to examine all of your sources of money. Revenue for a certain time period is shown, along with further product and customer breakdowns. You also get a table with details about your invoices, which you can filter by status, date, and customer.

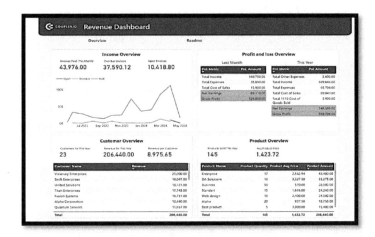

This QuickBooks revenue dashboard allows you to find out which products or services are doing well, how much money is flowing in, and where you might increase sales. The template may be used with either Power BI or Looker Studio.

QuickBooks's Accounts Payable dashboard

The Accounts Payable dashboard enables you to effectively manage your invoices and keep track of your outgoing payments. The quantity of bills paid and unpaid by the vendor, the age of accounts due, and a summary of the bank and cash balances are all shown.

With the help of this QuickBooks dashboard, which clearly displays your payment commitments, you can prevent late fines and manage your cash flow.

QuickBooks dashboard for accounts receivable

Get an accounts receivable dashboard in addition to the AP panel to monitor your incoming payments and guarantee on-time collections. This QuickBooks dashboard template shows the age of your receivables, the total amount of your accounts receivable, and a breakdown of your invoices that have been paid and those that have not. This tool allows you to see which bills are past due for a certain period of time.

With the dashboard, you can keep an eye on past-due bills, prioritize collections, and improve your cash flow.

An explanation of the native QuickBooks dashboard analytics

We'll go back to QuickBooks Online's built-in dashboard, which provides you with a concise overview of all the activities occurring inside your company. It includes a collection of measures that make it simple to analyze your data and track the effectiveness of your operations. The dashboard will show when you first launch QuickBooks after signing in. If you are a new user, the dashboard will show blank data. However, the page will alter as you start adding transactions. "Home" and "Cash flow," two tabs, are shown on the dashboard.

The Home tab has a number of widgets that you will find. Shortcuts, Sales, Invoices, Bank Accounts, and Tasks could all be there by default. You may add or delete widgets as you wish.

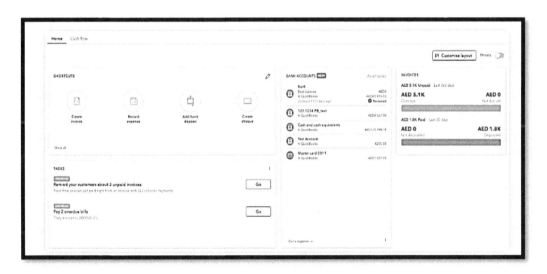

Setting up your business operations, such as browsing your account, personalizing your invoice template, and configuring your tax information, will be facilitated by the setup guide. You may save time on tedious tasks and rapidly access frequently used features in QuickBooks by using shortcuts. Examples of such responsibilities include the addition of a supplier, a bill, a cost, and a new customer. The balance for the current account you have linked to QuickBooks Online is shown under the bank accounts option. Under the Cash flow page, you can get a summary of your current cash balance, including the amount coming in from past-due and open invoices and the amount going out from the same bills.

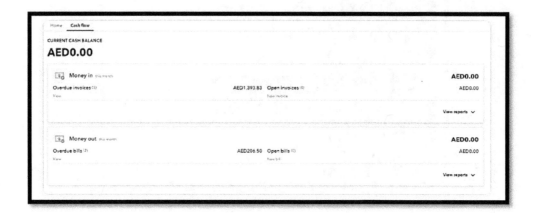

The main goal of the built-in QuickBooks dashboard is to draw attention to important financial information. This makes it simple to assess your company's performance. By the way, you can use the QuickBooks Online mobile app to monitor your finances from anywhere.

How can I personalize my QuickBooks Online dashboard?

The QuickBooks Online dashboard comes with a default set of widgets, but you may also rearrange them to display only the information that matters most to you. Click "Customize Layout" in the top right corner of the dashboard. Widgets may then be added, moved, and removed as necessary.

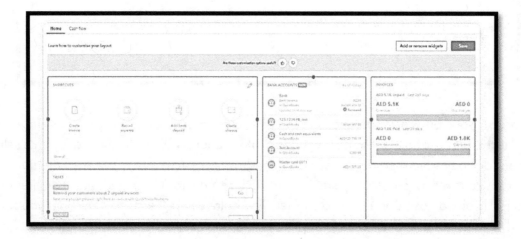

You may add the following widgets to your dashboard:

- Accounts Payable
- Accounts Receivable
- Bank Accounts
- Cashflow
- Expenses
- Invoices
- My apps
- Profit & Loss
- Sales shortcuts
- Tasks

This is how your QuickBooks Online dashboard will seem once all of the widgets are added.

Can I start from scratch and build a personalized QuickBooks analytics dashboard?

In QuickBooks, there is another method for creating a dashboard. You may add features and functionality to QuickBooks with a custom dashboard, making it more suited to your unique business requirements. The secret to creating a unique dashboard is automating

QuickBooks exports using Coupler.io. You may connect QBO to this reporting automation platform and input your data into the destination once you've arranged it in a spreadsheet or data visualization tool. **This is how it seems.**

⬇ **Gather data:** Click Proceed after selecting the destination (Destination) for your data's storage in the form below. The option to register for Coupler.io without supplying any payment information will be presented to you.

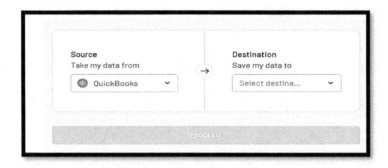

Next, choose which data fields (Account, Invoice, Payment, etc.) to export after connecting your QuickBooks account.

⬇ **Arrange information:** The next step is to convert the selected data set in order to get it ready for analysis:

➢ **One is able to:**
- Sort or filter data.
- Hide any unnecessary columns.
- Add new calculable columns, change the types of existing columns, or rename them.
- Integrate information from several sources, including applications, QuickBooks accounts, and other data entities.

↓ **Upload data and view it:** To connect to your destination, follow the in-app instructions when the data is ready. You may enable automatic data refresh if you want your dashboards to update automatically.

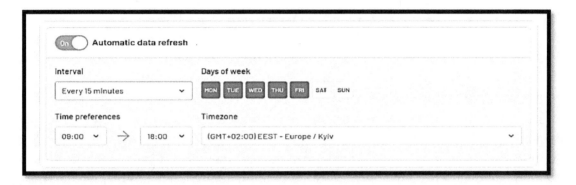

> After you import your QuickBooks data into a spreadsheet or business intelligence application, you have total control over how your dashboard is created. Coupler.io supports the following apps:
> - **Spreadsheet programs:** Google Sheets, Microsoft Excel
> - **BI tools:** Tableau, Qlik, Looker Studio, and Power BI

CHAPTER FOUR
BUILDING A COMPANY PROFILE

What does a QuickBooks company file mean?

A business file in QuickBooks is the main location for all the financial documents and information needed for accurate accounting and reporting. It includes essential components such a general ledger, chart of accounts, and customizable financial reports to assist users in monitoring their earnings, expenses, and financial health. You have easy access to all of your financial information in one convenient spot. The company file in QuickBooks makes it simple to handle invoices, payments, and payroll while enabling accurate recording and monitoring of all financial activities. The company file's extensive capability is essential for supporting essential accounting operations and facilitating well-informed financial decision-making.

Create a QuickBooks Online account with your company details

1. Compile business information and log in to QuickBooks

Before we begin setting up QuickBooks Online for your company, collect the necessary business information. **Although you should ideally have everything on this list, you may always make changes if needed:**

> - Business name
> - Address
> - Email
> - Website
> - Digital copy of your company logo
> - Federal employer identification number (EIN)
> - Business structure, such as sole proprietor or partnership
> - Accounting method (cash or accrual)

Now that you have all of your details, log in to your QuickBooks account. From your dashboard, click the gear icon in the upper right corner, then choose Account and Settings to see your account and settings.

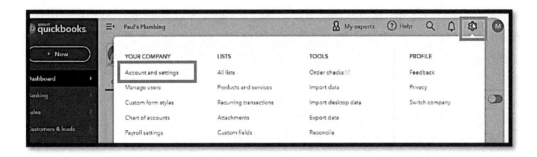

Go to Account and Settings to see the Company tab. Next, choose the Company option under Account & Settings. The five areas of the Company tab that need to be configured are Company Name, Company Type, Contact Details, Address, and Marketing Preferences.

2. Modify the Name of the Company

Changes may be made anywhere in the business name area or by clicking the pencil symbol. Click "Save" after you've finished modifying.

The firm name portion is divided into three sections, as seen in the figure above:

A. Company logo: Import your company's logo into customizable forms. Your logo should be saved as an image file on your computer. You may click on the gray square to add your logo. In the picture above, we have already uploaded the company's logo. To add another logo, just click the blue + sign, choose the file you want to upload, and then click Save.

B. Company and legal name: Please enter your company name precisely as you would want it to appear on all upcoming invoices and paperwork. The legal name of your business should match the name that is on file with the IRS. The legal name will appear, among other places, on payroll tax filings and Form 1099. If your legal name is different from the business name you want on your invoices, uncheck the box and enter your legal name.

C. EIN: Verify that your EIN corresponds to the one provided by the IRS. If you work for yourself, you may use your Social Security number. Because EINs are important, QuickBooks can require you to confirm your login before allowing you to see or modify the EIN.

Your Social Security number should not be used. Although self-employed taxpayers may use their Social Security number in place of an EIN, we highly suggest obtaining one. Click the green Save button after you have entered your company's name, logo, and EIN.

3. **Decide on the Type of Company**

You may click the pencil icon anywhere in the Company kind section to change the kind of company you wish to register, or you can leave the space empty. **Click the drop-down menu next to the Tax form field to select your taxable entity type:**

- **Sole proprietor:** A sole proprietorship is a business structure in which there is just one owner and operator. When reporting income or loss, use Schedule C (Form 1040).
- **Partnership:** Select the "Partnership" entity type when doing business with two or more individuals. Form 1065 is used to submit partnerships' income and loss statements.
- **S corporation (S-corp):** A company that elects to be an S-corp will report on Form 1120S and distribute corporate income, loss, and taxes to its shareholders.
- **C Corporation (C-corp):** Qualifying companies do not have their taxes passed through to their owners; rather, they are taxed separately. C-corporations utilize Form 1120 for reporting.
- **Nonprofit organization:** These companies work to promote social causes rather than earn a profit. They are free from taxes. They use Form 990 to record their annual activities.
- **Limited liability Company (LLC):** An LLC is a viable choice to think about if you're unsure whether to record your business as a partnership, S-corporation, or sole proprietorship.

Next, start typing the name of your industry into the Industry field. QuickBooks will then provide options depending on the information it discovers. QuickBooks asks you to choose an industry or leave it empty. Click the green "Save" button when you're finished.

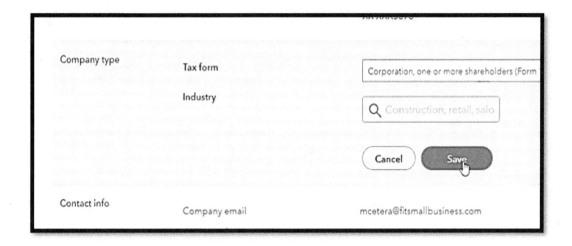

4. Revisit Your Contact Details

By clicking the pencil symbol or anywhere else in the Contact info section, you can enter contact details for both QuickBooks and your clients.

A. Email: QuickBooks will use the email address linked to your business to contact the QuickBooks administrator. The customer-facing email address will be shown on client invoices and other sales materials. If the address differs from the email address of the QuickBooks administrator, uncheck the box to input the correct address.

B. Company phone: Provide the number that will be used to contact customers with sales forms.

C. Website: Enter your website URL here to ensure it appears on all of your sales forms.

When you're finished, click the green Save button to continue updating your company's address details.

5. Modify the Address of Your Business

By clicking the pencil symbol or anywhere in the address column, you can add or modify your company's address. The corporate address, customer-facing address, and legal address are all located in separate sections of the most current edition of QuickBooks Online.

Address	Company address	355 Lexington Ave., 18th Floor, New York, NY 10017	✎
Address	Customer-facing address	228 1/2 11th Ave N, Texas City, TX 77590	✎
Address	Legal address	*Same as company address*	✎

- **Company address:** The address you use to pay for QuickBooks is the actual address of the business. Click "Save" after you've finished modifying.
- **Customer-facing address:** This should be the address that clients use to submit payments, and it will appear on your sales materials and invoices. Please include the correct address so that clients may check to see if it is different from the one your business uses. If the box is different, uncheck it. Click Save after you've finished editing.
- **Legal address:** You must use the address that is on file with the Internal Revenue Service as well as your legal address when filing your tax returns. Once again, if the legal address differs from the business address, you must input it and uncheck the corresponding box. Once the address has been entered correctly, click the green "Save" button to save.

6. Establish Communication with Intuit (Optional)

In the last step, you may work with Intuit, the company that owns QuickBooks, to personalize your marketing choices. You will be sent to Intuit's website after clicking on Marketing Preferences, where they will ask you a series of questions about how they may contact you. By completing the survey, you may choose not to receive any further emails, phone calls, or postal communications from Intuit.

Configuring permissions and users

You may add a user with a particular role in QuickBooks Desktop Enterprise to help you better manage your financial information. It is possible to establish a user with certain rights and obligations. The following are the steps to create a user and assign it a role. Note: Only administrators have the ability to create and manage users. Be careful to log in as the business file's admin user.

Add a user to QuickBooks

★ **Choose Company > Users > Configure Roles and Users:** QuickBooks will display the Users and Roles window box. This dialog box lists all of the users that have been given access to QuickBooks along with the permissions that have been provided to them. The user who is presently logged into the system is included in the list of users shown by the User List tab in the chat box.

★ **Press the "New" button to let QuickBooks know you want to add a user:** The New User text box appears in QuickBooks when you select this button.

★ **Provide a password and the user's identity:** Each person you are setting has to have their login credentials assigned. To do this, use a short name in the User Name area, such the user's first name. Once you've found the individual, enter their password twice: once in the Password box and once again in the Confirm Password field.

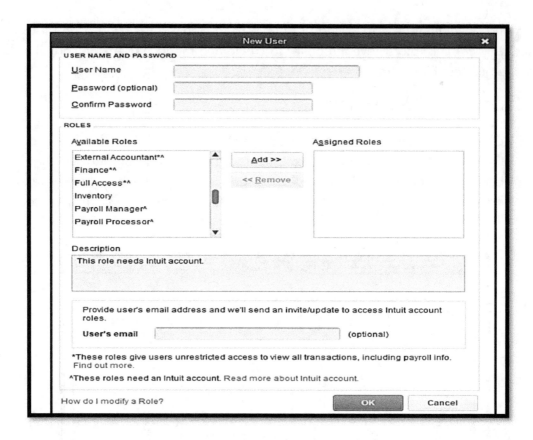

- **Determine the role or roles of the user:** The Available Roles list box allows the user to choose their obligations, sometimes referred to as duties. Next, click the "Add" button to add the chosen task to the user's list of responsibilities. The New User dialog box features a Description section at the bottom where you may provide further information about the position. To deactivate a user's employment, find their assigned position in the list and choose "Remove." For example, you may list the normal QuickBooks client type that would be given the chosen tasks.

- **(Optional) Switch roles as necessary:** With the help of QuickBooks, you may modify the tasks you provide your staff. To do so, go back to the Users and Roles box, choose the job you want to change, click the Job List tab, and then click the Edit button. Select an accounting activity or area from the list of Areas and Activities after QuickBooks has shown the Edit Role dialog box (not shown). Select the relevant radio buttons next to the Area Access Level to further define the permissions allowed to that position. The system will know that the user shouldn't be granted access if "None" is selected.

The "Full" radio option allows you to indicate that the user should have full access. To provide or deny the user access to certain tasks, choose the Partial button and then mark or unmark the View, Create, Modify, Delete, Print, and View Balance boxes according on your choices. To commit your changes to the tasks, click OK. This will bring up the Users and Jobs box again. Selecting an item from the Area and Activities list will allow you to see the default access levels for each job. The buttons and boxes in QuickBooks that match the Area Access Level display the current task arrangement. I think it's a good idea to restrict people's access to financial rules. You should choose "None" if someone isn't necessary to see the QuickBooks file on a daily basis. Only those who really need it, such those who need to create job quotes or invoices, should be given restricted access. Last but not least, the more freedom you give your staff, suppliers, or lawyers to alter your accounting system, the more likely it is that they will make errors. Furthermore, giving someone more power makes it easier for them to steal your money.

+ **Examine your user permissions (optional):** Make sure to thoroughly study the rights of the person you put up. Select the User List tab in the Users and Roles dialog box to get started. Lastly, click the Manage Permissions box after selecting the user. Click the Display button after selecting the user to open the View Permissions panel in QuickBooks. The dialog box (not displayed) will appear as a result. This box shows a long list of the things that the user cannot accomplish.

+ **(Optional) Examine your role changes:** You may need to verify your modifications after making a change to a user's permissions. To do this, click the Scroll Down button after selecting the task in the task List tab and entering the Users and Roles field. QuickBooks presents a new View Permissions box where you can view a list of the jobs you've given to both yourself and the program. Click the View Permissions option after selecting the jobs to see who has access to them. QuickBooks opens a new View Permissions window that lists all of the role-holder's restrictions and permissions.

⬧ You may click Close to end any open windows when you've completed verifying user and role rights. Click the Cancel or Close button to end any open dialog windows. For the new employee, this is their first chance to use QuickBooks. Their only rights are the ones you give them.

Advice: Depending on how often you recruit new employees and how you handle your books, you should review the rights every few months or annually. Your information must no longer be accessible to former workers or bookkeepers. They should be excluded from all professions! It's convenient that QuickBooks' access rights window allows you to access this data online. To print a tangible copy of the rights information, click the Print button on the window.

Adapting Enterprise Solutions' User Rights

The individual rights you grant are not set in stone. Go to Company > Users > Set up Users and Roles in QuickBooks Enterprise Solutions to open the Users and Roles text box (which is not visible). To begin, click this. Clicking the Edit button next to a user's name allows you to change their permissions once you've evaluated them. The Edit User dialog box that QuickBooks shows you resembles the New User dialog box, which you use to create a user and set their rights.

31

To change the user's information, complete the User Name, Password, and Confirm Password sections. You may change a person's QuickBooks rights using the Add and Remove buttons, the Available Roles list, and the Assigned Roles list. When you're done, click Close. You may think about adding a second user with the same set of permissions as the first. Find the person you want to clone in the Users and Role dialog box, and then choose Duplicate. Click OK when the Duplicate User window shows up after you've completed adding the new user to QuickBooks.

Alternatively, you may delete a person by using the Users and Roles box. Just choose a person's name and click the Delete button to get rid of them. QuickBooks will ask you for confirmation before allowing you to delete anything. Selecting "Yes" validates the user's removal from QuickBooks.

Modifying user privileges in QuickBooks Premier and Pro

In QuickBooks Pro or Premier, the powers you provide someone may be changed. To do this, choose Company > Set up Users and Passwords > Set up Users. This will bring up the User List dialog box.

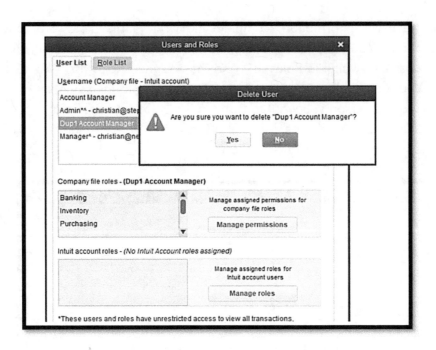

To see a user's permissions, choose them from the drop-down menu and click the see User button. When you do this, QuickBooks will display the View User Access text box. This provides the same information as the completed Set-Up User Access and Password dialog boxes. This is the box to fill up with the user's rights when creating them for the first time. Click the Leave button to close the View User Access window. After examining a user's permissions, select the user and click the Edit User button. QuickBooks uses the same set of dialog boxes that you would use to explain their privileges and establish an account. Using the Next and Back buttons, you may change the username or password, choose the user's degree of access, and, if necessary, limit their ability to do a particular QuickBooks job. Another conceivable usage for this box is to remove a user. Choosing a person and then choosing the Delete Person button will delete them. QuickBooks will request confirmation before removing. Selecting "Yes" validates the user's removal from QuickBooks.

Making Use of Audit Trails

When you allow other users to utilize the QuickBooks data file, the QuickBooks Audit Trail function comes in handy. It records the kind of changes made as well as who made them. This feature allows you to determine if the file has changed and, if so, who made the change. It never shuts off. Advice: Transactions may only be deleted from the Audit Trail collection of records by storing and reducing them. By selecting Reports > Accountant >

Taxes > Audit Trail, you may create an Audit Trail report. Note that the kind of adjustment and the name of the QuickBooks file user who made the change are shown in this report.

Facilitating Concurrent Multi-User Access

In certain cases, a single computer and the software are sufficient, even if several individuals use QuickBooks at work. One PC running QuickBooks may be enough for a small business with only the owner and an office assistant who have access to QuickBooks data. QuickBooks does, however, allow many users to view data files at once. It goes without saying that you should start by generating a number of users. If more than one person has been added, QuickBooks may be installed on numerous PCs. You may use any of the other QuickBooks installations to view the primary computer's QuickBooks data file if all of these PCs are connected to the same Windows network. You must also tell QuickBooks to do so if you want to let many users to use the program at once. Navigate to the File menu and choose "Switch to Multi-User Mode." Once you're finished, go back to File > Switch to Single User Mode to turn Multi-User Mode off.

Many people can use QuickBooks at once because of a feature called "record locking," which locks just the records you're working on and not the whole QuickBooks data file. With QuickBooks, it's perfectly okay if you'd want to work for Company A and someone else wants to work for Company B. But none of you can work for both Company A and Company B at the same time. For all of your tasks here, you may anticipate using the same client record. Note: In a multiple-user QuickBooks system, it is not technically permitted to utilize the same version of QuickBooks on several computers. For each computer with QuickBooks installed, you must buy a copy of the program. However, keep in mind that Intuit provides multi-user editions of QuickBooks. In this case, five licenses may be acquired for a single box of QuickBooks. QuickBooks Enterprise allows up to 40 users to connect to several networks at once. Previously, QuickBooks allowed up to five users to connect to several networks at once. If your sales people create bids or bills for clients, having a large number of QuickBooks users on staff may be advantageous. In this case, offering QuickBooks to each provider may be a smart move. It's important to keep in mind that these suppliers should only be able to make statements or, at best, create and print one rough invoice.

CHAPTER FIVE
ABOUT QUICKBOOK FINANCE MANAGEMENT

Creating Accounts

Follow the steps below to set up your QuickBooks account:

1. **Create your chart of accounts:** Your chart of accounts must be ready before you can start setting up your QuickBooks account. The chart of accounts provides specifics on how well your business can monitor its financial transactions. **These kinds of accounts are often categorized as:**
   - **Assets:** The things that your company possesses, such as money, inventory, and accounts receivable.
   - **Liabilities:** The debts owed by your company, such as loans and accounts payable.
   - **Equity:** The owner's stake in the company, such as retained profits.
   - **Income:** Sales and service revenue.
   - **Expenses:** The costs associated with operating the company.

2. **Go to the Accounts Chart**
   - **QuickBooks Desktop:**
     - Open QuickBooks and sign in to your business account.
     - From the Lists menu, choose the Chart of Accounts.
   - **QuickBooks Online:**
     - Log in to access your QuickBooks Online account.
     - Click on Settings (gear icon) to choose Chart of Accounts under Your Company.

3. **Add New Accounts**
   - **Launch QuickBooks Desktop:**
     - Select the Account button at the Chart of Accounts window's bottom.
     - Select New.
     - A bank, accounts receivable, income, or expense account are examples of the appropriate account types.
     - Click Continue to continue.
     - The information that has to be entered includes the account name, description, and balance, if any.
     - Press "Save & Close."
   - **QuickBooks Online:**
     - On the Chart of Accounts page, click the New button.
     - Select the relevant account type and detail type from the drop-down menu.

- ➢ If relevant, please provide the account name, description, and balance.
- ➢ Press "Save" and "Close."

4. Establish bank accounts

⬩ Desktop QuickBooks:
- ➢ To add a new account, follow the instructions.
- ➢ Select "Bank" as the account type.
- ➢ Enter the bank account information, such as the bank name and account number.
- ➢ Press "Save & Close."

⬩ Online QuickBooks:
- ➢ To add a new account, follow the instructions.
- ➢ Select "Bank" as the account type.
- ➢ Enter the balance and bank account information.
- ➢ Press "Save" and "Close."

5. Create accounts for income and expenses

⬩ Desktop QuickBooks:
- ➢ To add a new account, follow the instructions.
- ➢ Select "Expense" or "Income" as the kind of account.
- ➢ Enter the account details, such as the account name and description.
- ➢ Press "Save & Close."

⬩ Online QuickBooks:
- ➢ To add a new account, follow the instructions.
- ➢ Choose your account type from either income or expenses.
- ➢ Type the account information, including the name.
- ➢ Press "Save" and "Close."

6. Establish Accounts Payable and Receivable

⬩ Desktop QuickBooks:
- ➢ To add a new account, follow the instructions.
- ➢ Decide whether to use an account payable or receivable account type.
- ➢ Please fill out all the areas that are mandatory.
- ➢ Press "Save & Close."

⬩ Online QuickBooks:
- ➢ To add a new account, follow the instructions.
- ➢ Select the account type between accounts payable (A/P) and accounts receivable (A/R).
- ➢ After entering the information, choose Save and Close.

7. Establishing Accounts for Equity

⬩ Desktop QuickBooks:

- ➢ To add a new account, follow the instructions.
- ➢ Select "Equity" as the account type.
- ➢ If relevant, please provide the account name, description, and balance.
- ➢ Press "Save & Close."
- ⊹ **Online QuickBooks:**
  - ➢ To add a new account, follow the instructions.
  - ➢ Choose Equity as the account type.
  - ➢ After entering the information, choose Save and Close.

8. **Get Your Accounts in Order**
- ⊹ To improve the organization of your QuickBooks Desktop or QuickBooks Online chart of accounts, create sub-accounts. This facilitates the grouping of related accounts for better clarity.
- ⊹ When you follow the instructions to create an account, be sure to use the option to make the new account a sub-account of another account. A sub-account will be created as a result.

9. **Examine and Modify Account Information**
- ⊹ Regularly check your chart of accounts to ensure it is appropriate for your business.
- ⊹ You may modify accounts in QuickBooks Desktop's Chart of Accounts box by selecting modify Account with a right-click.
- ⊹ In QuickBooks Online, to make changes to an account, go to the Chart of Accounts page, click on the account, and choose Edit.

Advice for Account Creation

- ⊹ **Consistency:** Use consistent account names to avoid confusion and maintain organization.
- ⊹ **Relevance:** Only create accounts that have a direct connection to your company.
- ⊹ **Detail:** Account names and descriptions must to be sufficiently specific to allow for easy differentiation.
- ⊹ **Frequent Updates:** Keep your chart of accounts current by updating it whenever your company's operations or structure change.

The Reasons for Linking Bank Accounts and the Value of Proper Account Coding

Using your bank statement and QuickBooks Online, you may confirm the accuracy of your financial information. Your bank statement shows all of your company's actual financial transactions. By comparing your QBO data with your bank statement, you may identify errors, missing transactions, or irregularities. By taking these actions, you may ensure that the financial data you have in QBO accurately reflects your real financial transactions. Through bank reconciliation, you may discover errors or even questionable activity in your accounts. Inconsistencies between your bank statement and QBO data might indicate fraud or accounting errors. Early detection of these problems helps protect the financial stability of your company and prevent losses. Another fantastic feature of QuickBooks Online is the opportunity to examine your data in real-time from any place with an internet connection. Small company owners may now manage transactions, generate reports, and keep tabs on their financial information from any location. Using account types and detail types will result in correct data being shown in important financial reports. Use the appropriate account type if you want trustworthy reports, such as the income statement and balance sheet, to evaluate the financial health of your business. Finally, by connecting your bank or credit card account to QuickBooks Online, you may automate your accounting process and save time. Transactions no longer need to be manually entered. As soon as you join your bank account, QuickBooks will download and arrange all of your online bank transactions. This makes updating your bank feeds considerably simpler. All you have to do is review them and give your approval. You may also divide expenses among many accounts and firm sectors by using these data to automate the process of modifying transactions so they repeat themselves. Your task will be much easier as a result.

Documenting Transactions

Effective financial management is essential to a business's success. QuickBooks is a complete accounting program that makes it simpler to ensure accurate financial records and well-informed decision-making. It makes entering and keeping track of transactions more efficient.

Using QuickBooks to Record Transactions

+ **Recording Invoices:** Invoices serve as a record of the sales you have made to clients. To document an invoice:
    - Log in to access your QuickBooks account.
    - Select the "Invoicing" or "Sales" option.
    - Locate and select the "Create Invoice" or similar option.
    - Fill out the form with the client's details, the details of the service or product, the amount, and the price.
    - Kindly provide the conditions, due date, and mode of payment.

➢ Either print a copy of the invoice or save it and email it to the client.

✦ **Documenting Bills:** Bills are the sum of money you owe vendors. This is one method of recording bills:

➢ Navigate to QuickBooks' "Expenses" or "Bills" section.

➢ Choose "Enter Bill" or a similar option.

➢ Provide the vendor's information, prices, and deadline.

➢ The appropriate accounts should be used to classify expenses.

➢ When the due date approaches, QuickBooks will remind you to save the bill.

✦ **Tracking Payments:** When customers pay their bills, you need to record the following transactions:

➢ Proceed to the "Invoicing" or "Sales" area.

➢ Locate and stamp the client's invoice as "Paid."

➢ Among other things, the date and payment method need to be input.

➢ Assign the appropriate bank account to the payment in QuickBooks.

✦ **Tracking spending:** Monitoring Company spending is essential to accurate financial reporting.

➢ Go to the "Transactions" or "Expenses" area.

➢ Choose "Record Expense" or a similar option.

➢ Kindly include the date, spending type, payee, and payment method.

➢ Kindly provide all required documents or invoices.

➢ Put the money aside for later use.

Useful Advice for Precise Transaction Documentation

✦ **The key is consistency:** Create a consistent process to make reporting simpler and transaction recording more accurate.

✦ **Frequent Reconciliation:** Reconcile your bank and credit card accounts on a regular basis to identify and promptly address discrepancies.

✦ **Security of Data and Backup:** Make frequent backups of your QuickBooks data to prevent losing crucial financial information.

✦ **Make use of QuickBooks Support:** If you have questions or encounter issues, don't be afraid to call QuickBooks' hotline or support services.

Following these guidelines will help you record transactions in QuickBooks more accurately. Understanding this process is essential for making informed choices and promoting progress. It will significantly enhance your business's capacity for financial management.

Keep Track of QuickBooks Investments

Investing is a sound long-term financial strategy for both individuals and businesses. The popular accounting software QuickBooks offers a comprehensive solution to the challenge of accurately and successfully managing your money. By carefully recording them in QuickBooks, you can keep an eye on your earnings and expenses, track the performance of your assets, and generate insightful reports. Setting up your Chart of Accounts is crucial before you start entering investments into QuickBooks. The Chart of Accounts is a crucial tool for monitoring and planning your financial activity.

Documenting an Early Investment

Once you have created the appropriate investment accounts in the Chart of Accounts, you may start entering your first investment in QuickBooks. By doing this, you can ensure that your financial records accurately reflect the investments you have made. To input the initial investment, open QuickBooks and choose the Banking tab. Click "Make Deposits." to bring up the deposit window. This is where you will input the details of your first contribution. In the "Received From" column, choose the individual or payee associated with the investment. Depending on the kind of investment, either your given name or the name of your business may be used here. Find the bank account and choose it in the "From Account" column to begin the transfer of money for the first investment. This ensures that the bank account and the investment account accurately reflect the money transfer. The next step is to choose the specific investment account using the "To Account" selection option. Consequently, the correct investment account will be shown as the initial investment in your Chart of Accounts. Enter the date of the first investment in the "Date" field. This is often the date when the funds left the bank and first showed up in the investment account. To provide a brief summary of the purpose or details of the first contribution, fill in the "Memo" section with a relevant description or note. Having this information on hand might be useful for future reference and report writing. The last step is to enter the starting investment amount in the "Amount" column. Verify that it matches the original amount of money placed into the investing account. After filling out all the necessary fields, click "Save & Close" to record the first investment in QuickBooks. Once this is completed, the new investment account balance will be adjusted in your financial records to appropriately represent your original contribution.

Documenting Distributions or Dividends

Dividends or distributions are a common source of income from investments. Maintaining correct financial records and monitoring investment income, such as stock dividends or mutual fund distributions, depend on accurately entering these transactions in QuickBooks. For the purpose of recording dividends or payouts, open QuickBooks and choose the Banking option. Select "Make Deposits." Enter the right information in the "Received From" field to indicate who provided the dividend or payout. Choose the investment account that will receive the dividend or payment in the "From Account" column. Enter the precise date of the dividend or payout in the "Date" section. Use the "Memo" area to give a brief summary of the dividend or payout, including any background information. Having this information on hand might be useful for future reference and report writing. Enter all of your dividend or distribution funds in the "Amount" field. Make sure you input the income amount accurately to reflect the money received. If taxes or withholdings are applicable to the dividend or payout, you may split the deposit in half by clicking the "Split" option. After that, you may allocate the money among the several accounts, including taxes and fees. After you've entered all the necessary data, click the "Save & Close" button to record the dividend or payout in QuickBooks. This modifies the amount in your investment account and shows the additional funds that were received.

How to Use QuickBooks Online to Enter a Credit Card Payment

1. Getting into the Credit Card Register

Before you can record a credit card payment in QuickBooks Online, you need to access the credit card register. The credit card register allows you to examine and control every transaction made with your credit card. **To access the credit card register, follow these steps:**

- After logging in, see your QuickBooks Online dashboard.

- Navigate to the dashboard and choose "Banking" from the menu on the left.
- A thorough list of all your connected bank and credit card accounts will be shown on the Banking page. Locate the credit card account you want to record a payment to, and then click on it.
- You may see a comprehensive record of all purchases made with the selected credit card by clicking here, which will take you to the credit card register.

Once you have access to the credit card register, the following step is to enter the credit card payment transaction. Keep in mind that by linking your bank and credit card accounts to QuickBooks Online, you may configure automatic synchronization with them. This application improves accuracy and saves time by directly integrating your transactions into QuickBooks Online. If you haven't already, connect your credit card by selecting "Connect account" or "Add account" from the Banking menu and following the on-screen instructions. Once you have accessed the credit card register, you can now enter the credit card payment transaction in QuickBooks Online.

2. Entering the Transaction for Credit Card Payment

Once you have access to the credit card register in QuickBooks Online, you must enter the credit card payment transaction. Among other things, the amount, date, and method of payment must be noted. **The following are the procedures to enter a credit card payment transaction in QuickBooks Online:**

- Choose "+" or "Add transaction" from the credit card register.
- Select "Expense" from the option that drops down.
- In the "Payee" field, choose the company or person who will be the recipient of the credit card payment.
- Choose the "Payment method" that best fits your requirements using the drop-down box. A check, credit card, electronic transfer, or any other appropriate method may be used for this.
- Enter the date of payment in the "Date" field. It should display the credit card payment date.
- The "Amount" column has to include the amount that needs to be paid.
- If you need to add a note or any other information, you may utilize the "Memo" section.

After you have completed entering all the necessary information, you may choose which credit card account to use for the payment. Please confirm that the payment's date and amount are accurate by checking them again. This maintains the accuracy of your financial records and facilitates credit card account reconciliation. Now that you have entered the information for the credit card payment transaction, we may choose the credit card account.

3. Selecting the Credit Card Account

Select the appropriate credit card account in QuickBooks Online once the credit card payment transaction has been completed with the required payment information. For the payment to be correctly recorded and displayed, selecting the correct credit card account is essential. **Use these procedures to choose a credit card for the purchase:**

- In the window displaying the credit card payment transaction, locate the "Account" field.
- Click the drop-down menu and choose the relevant credit card account.

You may configure QuickBooks Online to manage all of the credit cards that your business utilizes. The correct account must be selected using the credit card that was used to make the purchase. To add a new credit card account to QuickBooks Online, choose "New" under the Chart of Accounts. Then, complete the necessary fields by following the on-screen directions. Create the account now if you haven't already. You must choose the appropriate credit card account when making a purchase in order to enable effective reconciliation of credit card transactions and balances. Now that you have chosen the credit card account for the transaction, we can proceed to inputting the payment information for individual charges.

4. Inputting Payment Information

After selecting a credit card account, the next step is to enter the payment details into QuickBooks Online. Assigning each credit card payment to a specific cost can help you keep track of and manage your payments more effectively. **The following are the procedures to input the payment details:**

- In the window displaying the credit card payment transaction, locate the "Category" field.
- To make the payment, click the drop-down menu and choose the relevant account category or expenditure.
- Just click the "+" or "Add a line" option to add other categories for the payment to be applied to.
- Indicate the sum for every category of expenses. QuickBooks Online will calculate the remaining amount automatically.

Correct payment data entry is essential for efficient financial reporting and expenditure tracking. Assigning the payment to appropriate expense categories makes tracking and analysis simple. QuickBooks Online makes it simple to allocate payments to many categories of expenses. One significant advantage is the ease with which credit card payments for a range of business-related expenses may be recorded. After inputting the payment information and submitting customer payments, if your situation requires it, you may go on to the next step.

5. Assigning the Funds to Particular Costs

Allocating the money to certain costs is the next step after entering the credit card payment details in QuickBooks Online. Allocating the cash such that they show up in your financial records can help you better monitor the expenses of your business. **You may use the following method to assign the money to certain expenses:**

+ Check the payment information you supplied, such as the spending categories and payment amount.
+ Verify that the payment amount equals the sum of the funds allotted for every category of expenses.
+ Double-check that the spending categories you selected correspond to the items you purchased with your credit card.
+ To make any necessary adjustments to the allocated sums or expense categories, just amend the payment transaction.

By linking each payment to a specific expense, you can monitor the financial flow of your business and the many ways your credit card is being used. With appropriate payment allocation, accurate financial reports, such as profit and loss statements or expenditure breakdowns by category, may be produced. You may use these reports to see how your business is performing financially. Now that you have successfully assigned the credit card payment to specific charges, we may go on to the next step of recording client payments, if that is applicable in your case.

6. Inputting Payments from Customers

In some circumstances, you may need to utilize QuickBooks Online to monitor consumer credit card payments. This step is crucial if your company takes credit card payments from customers for products or services. **The following are guidelines for recording consumer credit card payments using QuickBooks Online:**

+ In the window displaying the credit card payment transaction, locate the "Customer" field.
+ Select the client who made the payment by clicking on the drop-down menu.
+ Simply click "+" or "Add a new customer" to add a client whose name isn't already there.
+ Enter the payment amount in the "Amount" field.
+ If necessary, you may provide a message or other information in the "Memo" box.

You may keep an eye on accounts receivable and ensure that clients get the credit they are due by accurately documenting their payments. Finally, to ensure that your financial records are always correct, QuickBooks Online allows you to match up customer invoices with the corresponding credit card payments. Simply repeat these steps for every customer payment that has to be documented. Now that you have entered the client payment information, we can proceed to the last step of completing the credit card payment transaction in QuickBooks Online.

7. Complete the Transaction Using the Credit Card

As we complete the credit card payment recording in QuickBooks Online, you must complete the payment transaction to ensure your financial records are correct and comprehensive. **Please take these actions to complete the credit card payment transaction:**

- Verify that all information is accurate, including customer payments (if any), spending categories, payment amount, and payment method.
- Confirm that the information is accurate and matches the credit card payment that was really made.
- If necessary, you may choose to "Edit" or "Delete" the payment transaction.
- Save and end the credit card payment transaction when you've finished confirming everything is in order.

When you complete the credit card payment transaction, you can be sure that all of your financial records are up to date and correct. You may verify your credit card transactions at the register once the transaction is complete to see how they correspond with your statements. This will ensure that your financial records are correct and that all of your credit card transactions are documented.

CHAPTER SIX
ONLY FOR ACCOUNTING

Using diary entries in QuickBooks

One of QuickBooks' most sophisticated features is journal entries. You should finish them if you work with an accountant or have a lot of accounting expertise. Credits and debits may be manually entered, much as in the days of accounting. The majority of agreements do not need diary entries to be made. You'll often discover that QuickBooks' built-in features are more suited for managing tasks like processing payments and paying bills than using journal entries. Journal entries are used to fix mistakes or assess the asset's decline. They may also be used to move money between other kinds of accounts, such debt, equity, income, and spending.

Detailed Instructions for Making a Journal Entry in QuickBooks

A comprehensive tutorial on creating a journal entry in QuickBooks may be found here.

1. **Go to the journal entry:** Choose Journal Entry from the drop-down menu after selecting Pick + New.
2. **Enter Amounts and Choose Accounts:** The Account field appears on the first line. To choose the right account, use the drop-down menu. Here, your choice depends on whether you want to take money out of the account or add more. Whether you choose a credit or debit for the first account, be careful to enter the proper amount in the corresponding column (Credit or Debit). The journal entries will be immediately balanced by QuickBooks. On the next line, you may choose the second account that comes with the bundle. Enter the number in the other area once again to maintain the balance.
3. **Verify the equilibrium:** It is necessary to double-check the numbers. The sum in the Credit and Debit columns should be the same for each line. This guarantees that the journal is written objectively.
4. **Include Memorandum Details:** In your diary's "Notes" section, please describe why you are maintaining this specific entry. This note will explain the rationale for the entry when you and others check your data later.
5. **Save and Complete:** After you've gone over and double-checked everything, you have two options:
   + **Save and new:** By choosing the "Save and new" option, you may start a new entry in your journal right away and save your current one. Helpful when several entries are needed.

- **Close and save:** Choose this option to get back to QuickBooks' home screen after completing the journal entry.

Advice for Precise Journal Writing

- Ensure that you have a simple method for monitoring your diary entries. Keeping track of your funds will be lot simpler if you stick to a regular plan.
- Examine your diary entries on a regular basis to spot any mistakes or problems. Financial mistakes do not worsen if they are fixed quickly.
- In the "memos" area, specify the subject of every journal entry. Everything is now easy to verify and more open.
- If you are unsure about how to write in your diary, don't hesitate to ask an accountant or other financial expert for help. The better choice is to restart.

Revising Information about the Company

Journal entry for adjustment

Adjusting journal entries will be made using the client's QuickBooks Online business file.
- Visit and log in to QuickBooks Online Accountant.
- From the "Go to QuickBooks" drop-down option; choose your client's company.
- Press the plus sign.
- A journal entry needs to be selected.
- Next to "Is Adjusting Journal Entry?" check the box.
- Record the journal entry by following the instructions.
- Select "Save" and then "Close."

Examine and make adjustments to journal entries

Trial Balance Adjusted Journal entries may be reviewed and modified with the help of reports. In this report, find the sums of all the general ledger accounts before and after changing journal entries. **A list of all the entries is also available for updating.**
- Type "Adjusted Trial Balance" into QuickBooks Online Accountant's search bar. You may also choose to see the Adjusted Trial Balance report on the Reports page.
- Click "Customize" to adapt the report to your preferences.
- Confirm that the amount owed on all credit and debit cards is the same.

Using a transaction that has been committed to memory

Memorized (Recurring) Transactions is an option if you use QuickBooks and want to ensure that recurring purchases are documented. They may also help you remember certain facts that you need to type often. You may set automatic entries for certain time periods in QuickBooks. While QuickBooks Online calls it a standard transaction, QuickBooks Desktop calls it a saved transaction. This QuickBooks tool makes data input easier and more consistent. Additionally, it warns you of things you should not overlook, such those that could be important. This is best used to transactions in which the amounts involved stay consistent. If the sums do change, you may still create a method to verify them again, and the system will automatically fill in the rest. **The following examples may help you commit transactions to memory.**

- Customer invoices
- Depreciation expenses
- Insurance payments
- Payroll transactions
- Rent bills

Once the transaction has been created, make sure it is open on your screen in order to set up a remembered transaction. Remember to write down the class, amount, note, chart of accounts, and any other relevant information. In QBD, hold down the Ctrl and M buttons at the same time. The choices to automate and specify the time will appear on the next screen. It is not required to have transactions entered on a regular basis. You may always utilize your computer's Ctrl+T shortcut if you'd prefer not to enter them but still want to remember them.

In QBO, if you go to the bottom of the agreement and choose "Make Recurring," a window with more information will show up than the one in QBD. But the basic configuration doesn't change.

Remember to delete this action once it stops happening. If you keep it like way, the automatic input will continue even if you don't.

Examining the tax and accounting report

Select Reports and then select that option to bring up the Accountant & Taxes page. Twenty reports and instructions on this submenu will be very useful and interesting to accountants. I've just provided images of the Trial Balance report in this section, although the Accountant & Taxes menu has many additional reports available.

The reports are listed as follows:

+ **Adjusted Trial Balance:** The Adjusted Trial Balance menu command may be used to create a Trial Balance report as of a certain date. This version of the Trial Balance report is different from the next one since it clearly shows the journal entries that need to be changed. The journal entries that need to be adjusted are the ones that were recognized as such. There is a checkbox for Adjusting Journal Entry in several versions of QuickBooks, including the one you often use. If you would want to make a changed entry in your journal, choose this option.

+ **Trial Balance:** The Trial Balance menu option, as expected, creates a report of the Trial Balance as of a given date.

+ **General Ledger:** By choosing the General Ledger menu command, you may create a report that only shows the accounts in your Chart of Accounts list and updates the account for the month, year, or any other accounting period you choose.

+ **Transaction Detail by Account:** The "Transaction Detail by Account" menu choice provides the anticipated information. Every action that affects a particular account is listed.

+ **General Ledger:** Upon selecting "Changing Journal Entries," either you or another user will be presented with a list of all journal entries that have been marked as changing entries.

- **Journal:** The Journal function in the menu allows you to create a report that breaks down events by kind and quantity.
- **Audit Trail:** For accountants, the Audit Trail report is very important. This is especially true for accountants who worry excessively about modifications to their work. In the Audit Trail report, activities are arranged by creator. The Audit Trail report provides a comprehensive record of all transaction changes along with the individuals who made them.
- **Closing Date Exception Report:** you eliminate any out-of-date accounting data, be sure you close the books at the end of the year. You will get a Closing Date Exception Report as a result. The Closing Date Exception Report tool may be used to find changes made to closed agreements.
- **Customer Credit Card Audit Trail:** This report is perfect for you if you have a lot of credit card transactions that you don't understand. It only shows transactions made using credit cards.
- One such command is "Voided/Deleted Transactions Summary," which creates a list of all transactions that have been rejected or erased.
- **Voided/Deleted Transactions Detail:** This command creates an exhaustive list of all transactions that have been canceled or removed.
- **Transaction List by Date:** This report provides a Transaction List by Date, showing transactions in the order they were entered.
- **Account Listing:** Each account in your Chart of Accounts is included in this report. In addition to giving you the account value, the report also shows you where on your tax return to include the account.
- **Fixed Asset Listing:** This report shows a list of every fixed asset in your Fixed Assets list.
- **Income Tax Preparation:** A report that lists the lines on which the account amounts appear on the tax forms will be shown to you as you prepare to submit your income tax return.
- **Income Tax Summary:** This report indicates which amounts should be reported on which lines of your tax forms based on the information you submitted while preparing your income taxes. All of your bank accounts will be checked by QuickBooks if you are a lone owner submitting a Schedule C tax return. The correct amount that ought to be recorded on the "sales" or "gross receipts" line of your Schedule C tax return is then shown when it has compiled all of the accounts.
- **Income Tax Detail:** This report provides the same information as the Income Tax Summary report, but it also shows the individual accounts that are added together to get the tax line total.

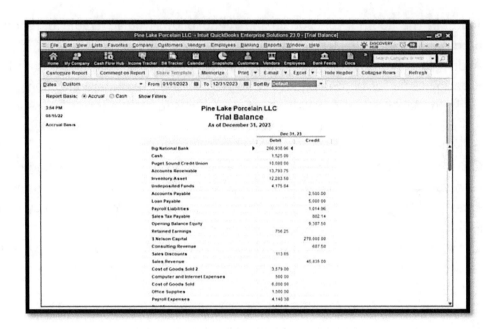

Making a duplicate of the QuickBooks data file for an accountant

In QuickBooks, an "Accountant's Copy" is a copy of your business file that you use to update your data while you're at work. Your QuickBooks Accountant file may be modified as needed, and it will be returned to you in a format that you can quickly integrate into your working company file. It's simple to integrate our work with your previous efforts once we provide you with the updated QuickBooks files. Only by providing us with an accountant's copy will these changes appear in QuickBooks right away.

To create an Accountant's Copy (.QBX), follow these steps:

- Press "File" first, followed by "Send Company File."
- Next, choose Client Activities, then Accountant's Copy, and finally, Save File.
- **Decide on a date for division:** You will have access to transactions that take place after the dividing date, and we will have access to transactions that take place before to that date. One method for completing year-end taxes is to use December 31 of the previous year as the separation date. If you want to report on financial changes every three months, choose the last day of the previous month or quarter.
- Press the following button.
- (Optional) Update the QuickBooks "Accountant's Copy" file's name and location. The file must finish with.qbx. The location of the Accountant's Copy may be specified by you. anything's usually preferable to save anything to your desktop

before uploading anything to your CMP Sharefile account, CD, flash drive, email attachment, or other given connection.
+ Click "Save."
+ After you have handed your accountant the.qbx file for the Accountant's Copy, go on with your task.

A Few Remarks While Producing the Copy

Once the accountant's copy has been saved, "Accountant's Changes Pending" will show up in QuickBooks' title bar. It will stay there until you add the accountant-made changes or eliminate the limitations. If you remove the constraints before the accountant returns the revisions, you won't be able to import them into QuickBooks right away.

How to Get Rid of Limitations

*The accountant's copy restrictions are permanently removed. Please note that doing so will make it impossible for you to import the changes you made to the current Accountant's Copy into your file. Before eliminating limits, you should make a copy of your notes and get assistance.

Follow these methods to get rid of restrictions:
+ Press "File" first, followed by "Send Company File."
+ Under Accountant's Copy, choose Client Activities.
+ Press the button to remove restrictions.
+ Verify, Yes, I do wish to remove the copy limitations for accountants. Click OK to finish.

Utilizing the Commands for Client Data Review

To access the Client Data Review-Start Review box, choose Accountant > Client Data Review > Client Data Review. A dialog box that explains how to clean up a client's QuickBooks file will show up when you click this button. Reclassifying transactions (helpful for correcting major errors), deleting undeposited money and faulty payroll liability accounts, writing off transactions, and locating and repairing unapplied customer and vendor payments and credits are some of the main issues it helps with. If you're using QuickBooks' Accountant Edition, these should be plenty to quickly manage a client's messy records. If you aren't using QuickBooks, you can only get a copy of the Accountant Edition by becoming a QuickBooks Certified ProAdvisor. Keep in mind that the Client Data Review tools are covered in great detail in the QuickBooks Certified ProAdvisor course.

CHAPTER SEVEN
UNDERSTANDING BUDGETING
Examining typical budgeting strategies

Examining common budgeting strategies in QuickBooks necessitates being acquainted with and adept at using the features and capabilities of the application for creating, tracking, and managing budgets.

A few tried-and-true techniques for making a budget that integrates with QuickBooks are as follows:

- **Make a thorough budget:** QuickBooks allows you to create comprehensive budgets by classifying various forms of income and spending. Establishing monthly or yearly goals for every area can help you develop a thorough plan for your financial operations.

- **Make Use of Past Information:** Utilize QuickBooks' past data to inform your budget creation. Analyze past financial performance to make informed predictions about future revenue and expenses. QuickBooks's reporting features may help with this examination.

- **Personalize Reports on Budgets:** QuickBooks provides customizable budget reports that allow you to examine how your budget and reality comparisons vary. These reports may be customized to emphasize certain time periods, departments, or projects, giving you important insight into how well you're sticking to your budget.

- **Keep an eye on cash flow:** Use QuickBooks to create cash flow-focused budgets. By doing this, you can keep an eye on your company's revenue coming in and going out and ensure that you have enough money to pay all of your expenses.

- **Make sensible objectives:** When creating budgets using QuickBooks, be careful to establish realistic and achievable objectives. This implies that the budget for your business will be reasonable and consistent with its available funds.

- **Regular Evaluation and Modifications:** Regularly examine your budgeting in QuickBooks and make any required adjustments. Being flexible enables you to modify your financial plan in response to your company's evolving needs, which is crucial in uncertain business environments.

- **Employ Classes and Subaccounts:** Two features in QuickBooks that may be quite helpful with budgeting are subaccounts and classes. While subaccounts allow you to break down large categories into more manageable subcategories, classes allow you to allocate spending to certain projects or areas of your business.

- ╋ **Automate Transactions That Recur:** Use the automation features in QuickBooks to handle transactions that occur often. By removing the need for manual data input, this method of incorporating regular income and spending into your budget may save you time and effort.
- ╋ **Using QuickBooks Online Advanced for Forecasting:** QuickBooks Online can anticipate your future revenue and expenses using sophisticated forecasting algorithms and historical data. Consider using these choices to improve the accuracy of your budgeting.
- ╋ **Work Together with Your Group:** QuickBooks allows for multi-user interaction, which makes budgeting easier for many teams or departments. Transparency is promoted and all relevant stakeholders are engaged.
- ╋ **Monitor and Manage Expenditures:** You may use QuickBooks to compare your budget and actual spending. Use this information to identify possible areas of overspending and put remedies in place to get your finances back on track. In conclusion, QuickBooks is an excellent tool for budgeting, and you may utilize your money more wisely by using these common techniques. Regularly reviewing, updating, and using QuickBooks' various features can improve the effectiveness of your business budgeting.

Adopting a pragmatic approach to financial planning

To exacerbate the situation, developing a budget for your business requires more effort than just enumerating all of your projected revenue and costs. Usually, a bank sheet is also produced. You can't make a balance-sheet budget while having breakfast in the morning before the kids wake up, or on the back of a cocktail napkin. You can make a simple, rough budget if all you have to do is monitor your earnings and outlays. For example, you may write down the anticipated sums for each account on the back of a napkin.

Making use of the budget setup window

You should enter your budget into QuickBooks after creating it. It's simple to create a new budget in QuickBooks by following these steps:

- ╋ **Select Set up Budgets under Company, then Planning and Budgeting:** QuickBooks shows the establish New Budget text box when you want to establish a new budget. Note: If you have previously created a budget, QuickBooks will show the Set up Budgets window instead of the text box for establishing a new one. Click the Create New Budget button in QuickBooks' Set up Budgets window to bring up the Create New Budget text box.

- **Decide on the fiscal year:** Select the year in which you want to adhere to your spending plan. To do so, just type the fiscal year into the text box given. You may change the year to 2021 using the buttons if your budget is for that fiscal year.
- **Choose between making a profit and loss budget or a balance sheet:** Click "Next" to proceed to Step 4 of creating a profit and loss budget after selecting the "Profit and Loss" radio choice. Select the Balance Sheet option from the drop-down box to generate a balance sheet budget, and then click Finish to go to Step 5. Recognize that the preparation of budgets for profit and loss statements and balance sheets differs. You estimate how much money the account will make or spend each month when you create a profit and loss budget. You plan for the entire amount that will be in each account at the end of the month, whether it be owner's equity, debt, or assets, in a balance sheet budget.
- Click Next after adding more profit and loss budget criteria in the Additional Profit and Loss Budget Criteria dialog box. Use the Customer:Job radio option to add Job information to your budget. Click the Class radio option to add Classes to your budget. Please use the No Additional Criteria radio option if you want to create a profit and loss budget in Step 3. Note: In order to budget by class, you must first enable class tracking.
- In the Create New Budget text box, choose whether to start from scratch or use already data for creating the budget. If you wish to start the budgeting process from the beginning, use the "Create Budget from Scratch" option button. If you want to base your budget on last year's actual figures, use the "Create Budget from Previous Year's Actual Data" option.
- **When you're finished, click Finish:** In QuickBooks, the Set up Budgets window appears.

How to operate on a budget that already exists

To modify an existing QuickBooks budget, follow these steps:
- **Select Set up Budgets under Company > Planning & Budgeting:** The budget setup window in QuickBooks opens. All of your projected monthly income and year spending should be included in this section of the budget.
- **Decide on or make a budget:** From the Budget drop-down menu at the top of the window, choose how much you want to work with. Simply click the "Create New Budget" option to begin over. You have an infinite amount of budgets at your disposal.
- **Select a client if you'd like:** Usually, a budget is made for each account. If you want to be more specific with your budget and estimate amounts for jobs, courses, or customers in general, use the "Current Customer:Job" drop-down option to

select specific clients from whom you expect to make or spend money. **Note:** Unless you explicitly choose to budget by customer when you established it, the Customer:Job drop-down choice will not appear in your budget.

✦ **Put the allocated amounts for each month of the year in writing:**

➢ In the box on the right, type the monthly amount you want to spend on each account. Remember that each account's monthly revenue and expenses are estimated in the budget. Owner's equity, debt, and asset levels are based on projected monthly account balances.

➢ You may move the desired amount from one month to the next by selecting the Copy across option.

✦ **(Selective) Modify the number of rows:** If the year total for an account doesn't add up, you may either utilize the Add Row Amounts button or change the monthly amounts to equal one another. You may change the row amounts by using this button, which opens the dialog box shown in the accompanying picture. You may choose the month you want to start with by using the Start At drop-down option. It may be the first month or the one that is currently being chosen. To express a desired increase or reduction in the funds you have allotted, provide a monetary amount or percentage. When you're done, click OK to close the text box.

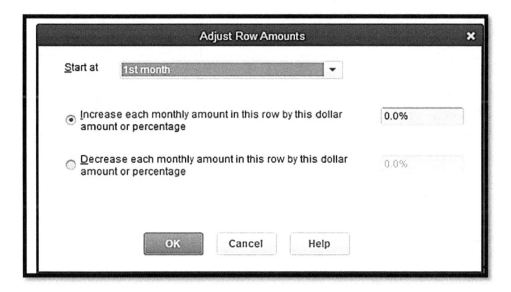

✦ **As needed, repeat:** Repeat Steps 3–5 to record restricted amounts in several accounts. I understand; it takes a lot of work. Few people spend most of their time annually handling scheduled data, despite the fact that many organizations employ hundreds or even thousands of workers.

A few last remarks on budgeting

As you complete your budgeting process, it is crucial to consider the significance of this financial planning activity. **To sum up, here are some considerations and comments to make for effective budgeting:**

- **Making Strategic Decisions:** your Company's long-term strategy and financial decisions are guided by a well-planned budget. With its assistance, you may more easily accomplish your company's objectives and make the most use of your resources.

- **Adaptability is essential:** Budgets provide structure, but flexibility is essential. A static budget may not be the ideal course of action for any particular organization due to the industry's constant change. Regularly assess your budget and make any required modifications.

- **Cooperation and Interaction:** Working as a team is necessary while creating a budget. Important individuals in your organization must participate. Everyone is more likely to follow the budget when everyone is aware of its goals and constraints.

- **Make the Most of Technology:** To make the process of setting a budget easier, utilize software like QuickBooks. You should consider automation, reporting tools, and integration choices if you want to make your budgeting more precise and effective.

- **Take Note of Variations:** The discrepancies between the budgeted and actual values provide valuable information. By learning what is causing your financial success and making the necessary adjustments going future, you may take advantage of these distinctions.

- Keep an eye on and evaluate "Budgeting" is the process of continuously planning for the future as opposed to only once. Regularly monitor your financial situation in relation to the budget. With this, you can see trends, address issues promptly, and take initiative.

- **Complement Business Objectives:** Make sure your budget aligns with your company's long-term goals before you establish it. Your long-term objectives, like as growth, lower costs, or more earnings, should be supported by your budget.

- **Inform and Engage Your Group:** A successful budget is one that your staff understands and supports. Ensure that key members of the team are aware of the goals, the budgeting process, and how they can help achieve them. This kind of involvement promotes pride and responsibility.

- **Celebrate Your Successes:** Make sure to rejoice when you reach or surpass your budgetary goals! Public recognition of achievements helps to boost morale and promote a sound financial culture.
- **Ongoing Enhancement:** Budgeting is a dynamic process. Adopt a mindset that always aims to improve. Analyze the effectiveness of your budgeting techniques, seek some input, and search for methods to make your approach better for the next budget cycle.
- **Managing Risk:** When creating a budget, consider potential risks and uncertainties. If you've planned ahead and put risk mitigation and contingency processes in place, your business can withstand abrupt changes in the market without endangering its financial stability. A well-written budget is a strategic tool for guaranteeing your business's long-term survival, not just a collection of figures. Developing financial growth and resilience calls for a methodical, flexible, and learning-focused approach.

Definition of financial forecasting, seven techniques, and how to use them

You should look into forecasting if you want to know when you may anticipate receiving the funds you need to generate revenue or grow your business. A financial forecast helps convince lenders or investors that their funds will be used wisely if you need to get money from them. Reliable forecasting may be used internally to prepare for your new company's budget and track your progress. Unlike financial forecasts, financial forecasting is a technique for projecting future profits and expenses using historical data and organizational assumptions. **It is essential for a number of reasons, including:**
- Making a pitch to potential investors to participate in your company in return for a portion of your future earnings
- Creating long-term budgeting and maintaining steady financial flow
- Using projected future cash flows as a foundation, look for investment money from a bank or other lending institution. Keeping stakeholders informed about the company's prospects and future
- Remember that financial forecasting is not the same as budgeting or financial modeling.

Comparing financial modeling and financial forecasting

Financial modeling and forecasting are two distinct concepts in the field of finance. Financial forecasting is the process of estimating future financial performance. Financial modeling is the process that results in a quantitative representation. Excel spreadsheets and financial forecasting software are popular modeling tools, and many of these applications work with QuickBooks. Financial modeling adopts a more comprehensive approach than other model types by taking into account several potential outcomes for a company's financial performance.

Budgeting vs. financial forecasting

Financial budgeting is a method for organizing your spending. Your budget is a separate document even if it could be based on your financial forecast. You must examine your forecasting and budgeting if you want to determine how much money you will have in the future. After that, you plan to use budgeting to allocate those resources and money. Let's say your financial prediction indicates that revenues will rise by $25,000 this year. To choose how to spend money, you might create a budget, such as $15,000 for new equipment and $10,000 for marketing.

Which techniques are used in financial forecasting?

Your company may benefit from seven primary methods of financial forecasting, each of which has nuances that might help you see your financial future. Both quantitative and qualitative methods are used.

Quantitative financial forecasting Techniques

These make use of historical data and figures and are often referred to as statistical forecasting. For example, forecasting revenues for the current quarter only based on sales from the prior year, disregarding external expectations like market sentiment.

Qualitative financial forecasting Techniques

The qualitative financial forecasting techniques are a little more complex. When formulating forecasts, researchers might include both hard and soft data. A qualitative prediction may depend on estimates, subjective assessments, and other less tangible factors in place of actual facts.

Of the seven methods for financial forecasting, two are qualitative, while the first five are quantitative. **Here they are:**

1. **The percentage of sales**

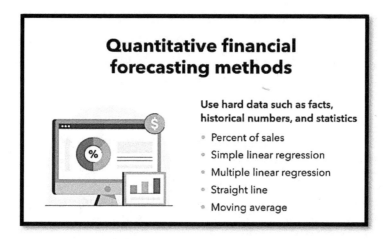

The percent of sales forecasting technique is used to predict each budgeted item as a percentage of sales. It is wise to use the same growth rate estimate for both as sales and the cost of items sold are predicted to rise in direct proportion. Examining your previous financial statements can help you determine the percentage of sales. By dividing the total sales by the accounts, this may be found. **The percentage of sales is broken out as follows:**

Percent of sales forecast		
	Amount	**Percent of sales**
Revenue	$90,000	100%
Cost of goods sold (COGS)	$36,000	40%
Gross profit	$54,000	60%
Operating expenses		
Sales and marketing	$9,000	10%
Research and development (R&D)	$6,300	7%
General and administrative	$13,500	15%
Total operating expenses	$28,800	32%
Operating income	$25,200	28%
Interest expense	$1,800	2%
Income before taxes	$23,400	26%
Income tax expense	$9,900	11%
Net income	$13,500	15%

For the sake of estimating in the future, let's assume that the cost of goods sold has consistently been 40%.

2. **Simple Linear regression:** The straightforward linear regression forecast technique is a popular statistical tool for determining the kind of association between two variables. Using the historical values of one variable (the independent variable) to make informed assumptions about the future values of another (the dependent variable) is helpful when creating a financial forecast. The foundation of basic linear regression is the assumption that the two variables have a linear relationship.

3. **The use of multiple linear regression:** When two or more variables have a major influence on an organization's performance, business leaders might use multiple linear regressions. This method enables more precise forecasting as it considers a number of variables that affect performance. For multiple linear regressions to be used for forecasting there must be a linear connection between the dependent and independent variables.

4. **Straight line:** The straight-line approach is predicated on the idea that a company's historical growth rate will be constant. A popular method for projecting metrics like future revenue or gross profit is to multiply the company's sales from the prior year by its growth rate. For instance, straight-line forecasting makes the assumption that the 15% growth rate from the prior year would continue into the next one.

5. **Moving Average:** The moving average approach employs the average or weighted average of previous periods to predict future ones. Because it focuses more on a company's demand peaks and troughs, this method works well for short-term projections. You can forecast the sales for the next quarter by averaging the sales from the preceding one.

6. **Market Research**

A qualitative approach that is crucial to organizational planning is market research. Company leaders may get a market perspective via the use of surveys, consumer trends, market conditions, and competitive dynamics. Market research might be quite helpful for startups without any historical data yet. New businesses might benefit from financial forecasting as it aids in budgeting for the first month and investor outreach.

7. **The Delphi technique:** The Delphi technique asks industry experts for their thoughts on current trends and prospects in order to predict how well a firm will do in the future. You may send them questionnaires to gain their expert advice on how your business will do.

Types of financial forecasting

There are many different types of financial projections, including both qualitative and quantitative methods. Financial forecasting techniques use historical data, present market conditions, and management insights to try to predict future financial outcomes. Furthermore, each category of financial forecasting indicates a different financial component. There are four different types of projections in the financial industry:

1. The Sales Forecast

A sales forecast may be used to estimate your sales for at least three fiscal years. It may be monthly during the first year and quarterly throughout the next two.

This kind of prediction provides solutions to queries like:

- *How many clients are you anticipating?*
- *How many units are expected to be sold?*
- *How much does it cost to sell goods?*
- *What will your product prices be?*

Sales predictions may be used to predict revenue. When you add include in the cost of goods sold, you can calculate the gross profit for each of those years. After accounting for your operating costs, you may calculate your net income (or profit) by subtracting these from your gross profit. When figuring your operating expenditures, start with your spending budget.

2. Expense forecast

Operating expenditures are any costs incurred by a business as a consequence of conducting its daily operations. Rent for your physical location and marketing fees are examples of both fixed and variable expenses to take into account. **The expenditure forecast model may be used to:**

- *Plan for both short-term and long-term financial demands using data from previous quarters or years.*
- *Be ready for unforeseen costs that can arise.*
- *Keep an eye out for subscription fees and other recurring expenses.*
- *As a consequence of operations and production, expect expenses to increase.*

General numbers will suffice, but a detailed inventory of office chairs and their prices is not required.

3. Forecasting from the top down

A top-down forecast considers the market as a whole when estimating future events. Using this method, you may create a top-down image of the company by taking into account each component separately. **For example, if you were in the auto parts industry, you would:**

- *Examine the automobile sales market as a whole*
- *Focus on used vs. new cars and*
- *Further refine it to the make and model of the components you must manufacture.*

This approach is often used by new businesses that don't currently have a lot of historical data.

4. Forecasting from the bottom up

The bottom-up prediction is utterly ineffective. In reverse, you start at a high level of abstraction and work your way down. **As an example, consider this scenario:**

- *Begin with the good or service you provide*
- *Work your way up to see the market for it as a whole.*

This approach is more complex than a top-down projection as it uses the company's historical performance to determine how well it will do going forward. It may be an extra step, but it is definitely worth the effort to collect and arrange your company's historical data.

How to make a financial forecast in five steps

One of the five processes in creating your financial projection is creating a set of pro forma financial statements.

1. **Obtain your previous financial records:** To develop accurate estimates, it is necessary to look at the company's historical success rather than making assumptions. Examining your company's historical financial records is essential to tracking its development and projecting its success in the future. Your accounting software has the ability to produce financial statements. However, make sure your accounting is up to date. After you have updated your records and accounts, you will be in a better position to make financial plans.

2. **Determine the purpose of your predictions"** Identifying the goal and kind of your prediction is the next stage. **Ask questions such as these:**
   - *What are you hoping to learn?*
   - *Would you want to know how many units of your service or product you can anticipate selling?*
   - *How much will the present budget influence the company's future?*

The next step is to choose a forecasting horizon, which may range from a few weeks to many years (although most businesses only plan for a year). For your internal financial predictions, you should prepare pro forma statements that look six months to a year into the future. When presenting your prediction to a lender or investor, you should generate pro forma statements for the next one to three years.

3. **Select a technique for financial forecasting:** With your prior financial statements and goals in hand, you must decide on a financial forecasting strategy. **Remember that:**

➤ Historical data and information may be used in quantitative forecasting to identify trends and patterns. Qualitative forecasting makes use of expert opinions and insights.

➤ Each approach is effective in a number of circumstances. A qualitative method is more suitable when there is no past financial data available, as is the situation with a startup.

4. **Make your pro forma financial statements:** After gathering information for your prediction, the following step is to create pro forma statements. For internal use or for completing a quick prediction, a pro forma income statement may be enough for businesses.

Pro forma income statement

	Year 1 (actual)	Year 2 (forecast)	Year 3 (forecast)	Year 4 (forecast)	Year 5 (forecast)
Revenue	$100,000	$120,000	$144,000	$172,800	$207,360
Cost of Goods Sold (COGS)	-$40,000	-$48,000	-$57,600	-$69,120	-$82,944
Gross Profit	$60,000	$72,000	$86,400	$103,680	$124,416
Operating Expenses					
Sales and Marketing	-$10,000	-$12,000	-$14,400	-$17,280	-$20,736
Research and Development (R&D)	-$5,000	-$6,000	-$7,200	-$8,640	-$10,368
General and Administrative (G&A)	-$15,000	-$18,000	-$21,600	-$25,920	-$31,104
Total Operating Expenses	-$30,000	-$36,000	-$43,200	-$51,840	-$62,208
Operating Income	$30,000	$36,000	$43,200	$51,840	$62,208
Interest Expense	-$2,000	-$1,800	-$1,600	-$1,400	-$1,200
Income Before Taxes	$28,000	$34,200	$41,600	$50,440	$61,008
Income Tax Expense (30%)	-$8,400	-$10,260	-$12,480	-$15,132	-$18,302
Net Income	**$19,600**	**$23,940**	**$29,120**	**$35,308**	**$42,706**

When providing the financial projection to lenders or investors, each financial statement should be included.

5. **Keep an eye on your outcomes:** Reviewing pertinent financial data on a regular basis can help you determine how accurate your financial projections are. You may determine how accurate your predictions were by comparing them to the actual results. Regular monitoring and analysis may lead to more accurate financial forecasts.

Forecasts may be created and managed in QuickBooks Online

Construct a forecast

While you may make predictions at any time, many people believe that the end of the year is a great time to start planning for the next year. You must be an administrator or a Standard All user in order to create a new prediction. **Note:** Please be advised that only those with an advanced QuickBooks Online subscription may see forecasts. If you're using a different subscription but still want to use Forecasts, learn how to switch the version of QuickBooks Online.

1. **Examine the business's fiscal year:** Make sure that QuickBooks is configured to start the fiscal year on the right day. Although you may create a forecast at any time, it is useful to start it at the start of the fiscal year.

---

1. Sign in to your QuickBooks Online Account.
2. Navigate to **Settings** ⚙, and then choose **Account and settings**.
3. Pick the **Advanced** tab.
4. Look at the field labeled **"First month of the fiscal year"** in the Accounting section. If it's wrong, choose **Edit** ✎.
5. After you've chosen the month you need, click the **"Save"** button.

---

2. **Obtain your forecast data:** If your data is already in QuickBooks, skip this step. In this scenario, you are able to base your projection on either this year's or previous year's fiscal facts. Before utilizing historical data, run a Profit and Loss Detail report to confirm that accounts and transactions are accurate. All of the transactions made so far this year will be included in the report. To examine the transactions from a prior fiscal year, the report must be modified.

3. **Make a forecast:** Note that the projected accounts list in QuickBooks Online is based on your chart of accounts. Update your chart of accounts to reflect any new accounts that may be needed before developing the projection. You may create a forecast using the financial information you have in QuickBooks Online. **First, if this is your first forecast:**

- After deciding on financial planning, choose forecasts.
- Decide to make a prediction.
- From the Forecast for option, choose the time frame for which you are forecasting.
- **Using the Forecast menu, choose one of the following forecasting methods:**
  - ➢ Average of Actuals
  - ➢ Data from the previous fiscal year (**Keep in mind:** Before saving for the first time, you may modify the forecast length and technique in the Settings panel).
- If you selected Average of actuals, choose the period of the prior actual to be used in calculating the average from the Use actuals dropdown option.
- If you want to set rules at the account type level, add rules (increase or decrease) under the Set rules section.
- When you're finished, press the Next button.
- By selecting the edit ✎ sign, you may modify the forecast's name if needed.
- When you're done, click Save and close to end the session.

Note: Click the Refresh actuals ↻ button each time you view the forecast to ensure it is current with the most recent actuals.

Modify a forecast

Make the required changes to a QuickBooks forecast.
- After deciding on financial planning, choose forecasts.
- In the Action column, locate your forecast and choose View/Edit.
- The choices are Save and Close or Save.

Footnote: Click the Refresh actuals ↻ button each time you view the forecast to ensure it is current with the most recent actuals. Additionally, you have the ability to modify each account on a monthly basis.

Create a budget from a forecast

- After deciding on financial planning, choose forecasts.
- When you find your prediction in the list, choose View/Edit in the Action column.
- Click on Make this budget to choose the fiscal year for the budgeting period.
- Select "make this a budget again" to save the prediction as a new budget.

Eliminate a forecast

- After deciding on financial planning, choose forecasts.

- Locate your forecast in the list, and then choose the Action column's View/Edit dropdown option.
- From the View/Edit dropdown option, choose Delete.

Note: Forecasts that have been erased cannot be retrieved.

Personalize a report

- Select Reports.
- Locate and choose the Profit and Loss Detail Report.
- **From the Report period dropdown box, choose a time frame. Consider this instance:**
  - ➢ If you would like to see data from a previous year, choose Last Year.
  - ➢ If you want to use data from the current fiscal year, choose This Year-to-date.

Take note: The start and end dates should align with your fiscal year.

- Select the Run report.
- To print or download a copy of the report without having to open it again, use the print or export icon.

CHAPTER EIGHT
SYNOPSIS OF CAPITAL BUDGETING
A Brief Overview of Capital Budgeting Theory

Capital budgeting is the intricate process managers use to determine a company's long-term investments or capital expenditures. In a word, it includes everything related to planning, assessing, choosing, and managing financial investments. The simplest aspect of this process involves obtaining funds, sometimes in the form of long-term finance, to buy assets, also known as capital goods. Facilitating the creation of long-term cash flows, often for years beyond the present, is the aim when choosing these assets. What kinds of investments are most often included in capital budgeting? These include replacing outdated assets and launching new or existing product lines. Because it is so important to investment decision-making, which centers on the wise long-term distribution of money to meet an organization's overall goals, capital budgeting is very complex. Since capital budgeting has a greater influence on a company's value than finance choices, it is an essential but difficult job for managers to do. The core of financial management is the interdependence of financial and investment decisions.

A company's long-term goals form the basis of capital budgeting, which makes it an essential part of any all-encompassing strategy. This lays out the group's plan for achieving its long-term objectives. The amount of money a firm spends on capital assets affects its performance, market position, and prospects. Capital investments may be challenging to convert into more flexible assets as they bind large amounts of money for long periods of time (Migliore and McCracken, 2001). They could also be difficult to remove. Furthermore, poor capital planning may seriously jeopardize a company's long-term existence. Because it is a thorough and intentional process, capital budgeting is an essential component of financial management. Its focus on long-term value creation, which is in line with the organization's strategic objectives, has a significant impact on a company's future performance and direction. Since of its intricacy, making wise decisions is even more important since mistakes in this area may have long-term effects on the whole firm.

The Rate of Return on Capital Calculation

The Rate of Return on Capital (RORC), one of the most basic financial metrics, indicates how lucrative a business is in relation to the capital it invests. This ratio is important for management and possible buyers since it shows how well the business converts money into profit.

The following formula may be used to determine the rate of return on capital:

$$RORC = AverageCapitalEmployed / NetOperatingProfitAfterTaxes(NOPAT)$$

Where:
- The abbreviation "NOPAT," which stands for "Net Operating Profit after Taxes," represents net operating profit after taxes.
- AverageCapitalEmployed displays the average amount of capital invested in the company during a certain time period.

The following are the steps to determine the rate of return on capital:
- **Calculate NOPAT or net operating profit after taxes:** To determine NOPAT, first subtract the operating profit of the business. Subtract the tax expenditure from the operating profit to account for taxes. The resulting NOPAT displays the corporation's after-tax income ratio.

Operating Profit — Tax Expense = NOPAT
- **Determine the Average Capital Used:** Capital Employed is the total amount of money that has ever been invested in a firm. It includes both long-term debt and fair value. The capital expenditures at the start and finish of a given time may be added together, and the total can then be divided by two to determine the average capital expenditure.

CapitalatStart+CapitalatEnd/2 = AverageCapitalEmployed
- **Determine RORC Using the Formula:** RORC is calculated by dividing NOPAT by Average Capital Employed.

Average Capital Employed/NOPAT = RORC
- **Interpretation:** Since the company is generating more money than it has spent on capital, a higher RORC shows that it is using its resources more effectively. On the other hand, a low RORC might mean that the company isn't making enough money off of their investment.
- **Examine Industry Standards:** When assessing the anticipated RORC, take past performance and industry standards into account. By comparing a company's RORC to industry standards, one may have a better understanding of its financial health and competitiveness.
- **Keep an eye on trends:** Create a routine for tracking RORC throughout a range of time periods in order to spot trends. The effectiveness of the company's cash

allocation may be seen by the steady movement of RORC. Lastly, figuring out the Rate of Return on Capital is a critical component of the financial analysis. This measures a company's ability to turn a profit in relation to its capital expenditures. This gives business owners important information on how well the company's financial and business initiatives are working.

Assessing Liquidity

The payback time, which calculates how long it takes an investment to provide a return equivalent to its original investment, is a simple indicator to employ when evaluating liquidity. Assume that, rather than using the example of the office building, you are thinking about a $10,000 investment that generates $2,000 in net cash flows per year. This will make the math a bit simpler. **Here, the following formula may be used to determine the payback period:**

Payback period = initial investment/annual cash flow
Here we detail an investment of $10,000 and the actual formula is $10,000/$2,000 = 5

The $10,000 may be paid back over five years thanks to the $2,000 yearly cash flow. Once again, liquidity is not a cause for worry. Generally speaking, liquidity is more important than money production. Making money is important, but you should routinely take liquidity very seriously as well. Sometimes it may be better to make investments with a greater rate of return. You'll have many of chances to reinvest when the investments do turn a profit.

Consideration of Risk

Risk is crucial: Bank CDs and other simple investments are not risk-free. However, if a capital purchase goes awry, no government body will defend your rights or make restitution. When it comes to capital investments, consider how you will assess and manage risk. **I think the following three things need to be emphasized:**

- When generating cash flows, use extreme caution and consideration. More accurate and useful predictions will come from a better analysis and assessment of the cash flows from a capital investment. You can precisely compute rates of return with accurate cash flow estimates.
- Try new things. You have to put your beliefs to the test. It would be prudent to test out various changes and keep an eye on how they affect cash flow and ROI. What

ultimately happens to the ROI when growth and inflation both slow down? It would be interesting to see it happen. A 2% inflation rate would have a significant impact on this company's cash flow and rate of return. The outcomes would be quite different if inflation had been 5% or 6% during the same 20 years. In the first case, things quickly go wrong. In the latter case, it is well known that in an inflationary climate, real estate investments backed by borrowed money may provide substantial profits, isn't that right?

- Consider the discount rate you apply. Think carefully about the discount rate you use. Even if I don't go into great detail regarding the discount rate, you should always consider the risk involved in a transaction. "Your discount rate should equal the rate of return that similarly risky investments produce." I often heard this fundamental rule from my financial professor, and it's very wise. Therefore, you should compare the possible benefits of a highly risky endeavor with those of more profitable but equally risky alternatives before committing to one.

You would never invest in anything that gave a lower return given the amount of risk involved. On the other hand, a lower discount rate is better suitable for less hazardous purchases. An office building is a very low-risk investment, therefore you wouldn't apply the same discount rate for a highly dangerous investment in brand-new, cutting-edge technology.

What is the connection between QuickBooks and all of this?

So, this is a query: What is the connection between QuickBooks and all of this capital budgeting stuff? To be honest, capital budgeting has nothing to do with QuickBooks. One of the most important aspects of financial management is capital budgeting. However, in this sense, QuickBooks isn't the ideal tool for the task. Additionally, keep in mind that you may estimate the savings you'll realize and the expenses of any capital projects you may be thinking about using a lot of the data you've gathered using QuickBooks. For example, one has to know their current rent expenses and any possible savings from buying the property altogether in order to make an educated choice about buying an office building. This kind of information is available in QuickBooks' comprehensive financial database. There is far more to cash flow prediction than what I have shown here. When making an investment in a building, it is prudent to account for the whole cost of upkeep and repairs. Think about all the costs involved with renting space from someone else, such the extra insurance the owner requires you to have or the money you'll need to pay since the space isn't ideal for your needs. QuickBooks makes it simple to find this kind of information.

CHAPTER NINE
APPLYING COSTING BASED ON ACTIVITY
Examining typical overhead allocations

Businesses must accurately calculate their overhead expenses in QuickBooks in order to determine how much it costs to operate a business and set competitive pricing for goods and services. Salaries paid to employees, rent, and utilities are examples of "overhead costs." Businesses must maintain accurate records of these expenses in order to assess performance across time and regions.

Comprehending the Overhead Rate Idea

When you look at all of your direct expenses over time, the overhead rate shows you what's left over. A number is shown. **The following are some common overhead costs for small businesses that use QuickBooks:**

- Rent
- Utilities like electricity and internet
- Administrative, marketing, and management salaries
- Software subscriptions
- Equipment maintenance and repairs

You must first add up all of your expenses for a specific time period in order to obtain your overhead costs in QuickBooks. Subsequently, divide that sum by your direct costs, which comprise labor and materials. This provides the overhead rate.

The Value of Precise Overhead Rate Estimation

It's important to keep accurate records of overhead costs in QuickBooks for a number of reasons, the most important being:

- **Make better pricing decisions:** Companies that know their true overhead costs and account for them in their pricing are better able to meet their profit goals.
- **Locate the cost centers:** Examining the overhead costs by department is one method to determine where the majority of your business's operational expenses are.
- **Benchmark performance:** It is simpler to control costs when comparing overhead rates across business units and over time.

Typical Overhead Rate: What Is It?

Overhead rates for small businesses can range from 20% to 60%, depending on the industry. A number of variables can affect overhead costs, including:

> - Facilities expenses from renting vs. owning
> - Regional cost of living differences
> - Technology investments
> - Economies of scale for larger companies

Examine the overhead rates to learn how to run your business more effectively. For small businesses hoping to use QuickBooks to boost their earnings, doing this step right is essential.

How is overhead calculated in QuickBooks?

QuickBooks uses your income and expenses to determine your overhead rate. The following easy techniques can assist you in comprehending and determining your overhead rate:
- Check Out Your Overhead Rate
- Select Profit & Loss from the Reports menu.
- You may see your income and expenses by scrolling down.
- Directly below that is the Overhead Rate, which shows the overhead cost as a percentage of income.

A company with $100,000 in total revenue and $20,000 in overhead expenses would be subject to a 20% overhead rate.

The Components of Overhead

Indirect costs of operations, like:

> - Rent
> - Utilities
> - Insurance
> - Office supplies
> - Salaries for support staff
> - Equipment costs
> - Accounting and legal fees

Therefore, by examining your overhead rate, you can rapidly determine how much these indirect expenditures are reducing your earnings.

The Significance of Monitoring Overhead Rate

Understanding your overhead rate enables you to:
1. Determine costs and prices.
2. Determine the possible profit margin for the goods or services.
3. Investigate ways to cut costs.
4. Consider market norms.

Thus, keep an eye out and act when the overhead becomes excessive. You'll earn more money if it's low.

What is the overhead rate formula?

The formula for the overhead rate is:

$$\text{Overhead Rate} = \text{Total Overhead Costs} / \text{Total Direct Costs}$$

Where:
+ **Total Overhead Costs:** This term refers to all of a business's secondary expenses, including rent, utilities, insurance, depreciation, and so on.
+ **Total Direct Costs:** This includes the costs of labor, direct materials, machinery, and any other expenses directly related to the production of the product.

Let's take an example where a company spends $1,000,000 on all direct expenditures and $200,000 on all overhead costs over a specific time period. **The overhead rate is as follows:**

$$\text{Overhead Rate} = \$200,000 / \$1,000,000 = 20\%$$

Using this overhead rate, the overhead costs are then allocated based on the direct costs spent by each department, product, service, project, etc. This means that if Product A's direct expenditures were $100,000; it would get $20,000 (20% of total overhead costs).

When calculating the overhead rate, the following factors should be taken into account:

- It makes it possible for a business to divide indirect expenses across several departments based on activity levels.
- Divide the entire overhead by the total direct costs for a specified time period to find the overhead rate.
- The rate may vary from one period to the next due to overhead and activity levels.
- Businesses may better understand their true costs and pricing with the help of an accurate overhead rate.

How is the amount of overhead allotted determined?

To figure out how much to enter for overhead in QuickBooks, you must first calculate your overhead rate. This can be done by dividing the entire number of hours you worked directly by the total overhead expenses for a specific time period. Assume that last month you had $10,000 in total overhead costs and 4,000 direct labor hours. Your overhead rate would be $2.50 per direct labor hour ($10,000 / 4,000 hours). For each hour of direct labor needed to manufacture or deliver your goods or services, this equates to $2.50 in overhead costs. **For a project or product requiring 100 hours of direct work, the given overhead would be calculated as follows:**
$250 is equal to 100 hours x $2.50 per hour.
The $250 would be the total cost of overhead for that specific task or item. When talking about the distribution of overhead expenses, it's critical to keep the following in mind:

- Indirect expenses like rent, utilities, administrative salaries, and so forth are included in overhead costs.
- Direct labor refers to employees who actively participate in the production process. Note these hours.
- The overhead rate must be routinely recalculated due to fluctuating expenses.
- Apply the overhead rate uniformly across all jobs and goods.
- An appropriate overhead distribution rate will help you better understand the expenses and revenues of your work, commodities, and services. This is essential for keeping costs and rates under control.

What is the applicable overhead formula?

Multiplying the allocated base by the designated overhead rate yields the applied overhead. Divide the anticipated total overhead expenses by the anticipated total allocation base to arrive at the designated overhead rate. For instance, the set overhead rate would be $2 per direct labor hour ($100,000/50,000 hours) if a company projects that it would spend $100,000 on overhead costs and hire 50,000 direct labor hours during that time. The allocation basis is the activity that establishes the overhead costs.

This activity often alludes to machine or direct labor hours. It's a tool for figuring out how much overhead each job requires. **The overhead for a job with a fixed rate of $2 per hour and 100 direct labor hours may be computed as follows:**

$2 per direct work hour is the predetermined overhead rate.

The jobs direct work hours total 100 hours.

Direct work hours x the predetermined overhead rate equals applied overhead.

= $200 ($2 per hour x 100 hours).

In this case, the work would incur $200 in overhead expenses.

The following is a summary of the formula:

Predetermined Overhead Rate x Allocation Base = Applied Overhead,

Where:

+ Estimated Total Overhead Costs / Estimated Total Allocation Base = Predetermined Overhead Rate

+ Allocation Base = Job-specific Direct Labor Hours or Machine Hours

A company may use this technique to assign overhead costs to certain professions based on the actions that produce those costs. This is an essential part in figuring out the overall cost of production.

Learning about ABC's operations

You must link your overhead costs to the goods or services you provide in order to create an ABC product-line income statement. Let's assume that the rent for the fictitious hot dog business is a significant issue since the chili pot needs an electricity connection to stay warm. You may also need an electrical connection to power the can opener you use to secretly open the chili cans you need to restock the pot. In this case, chili dogs and regular hot dogs cannot be used to split the rent. Reservations are required for chili dogs. The same reasoning applies to product prices. Instead, consider that the $1,000 in materials is just for a few napkins. Based on your observations, we may infer that the typical customer who buys a chili dog usually buys eight napkins (in case the chili sauce goes on their shirt), whereas the typical customer who buys a hot dog usually buys two napkins for their pet. This information might help you make the most of the $1,000 you spent on items. Take into consideration that this data shows that customers of hot dogs use over 4,000 napkins per day. Two napkins out of the 2,000 you've sold thus far have been utilized by every normal hot dog customer. 16,000 napkins have been used by customers who have bought chili dogs. I calculated this by taking the number of chili dogs you've sold and multiplied it by the eight napkins each client used.

The proportion of the total cost of the items that were used by frequent consumers of chili dogs and hot dogs, respectively, may be ascertained using the napkin use statistics.

Regular hot dog patrons will get 20% of the 20,000 napkins if they utilize 4,000 of them. $200 is equivalent to 20% of $1,000 in goods expenses. Therefore, $200 must be allocated to the standard hot dog line's supply expenses. You may split up some of the cost of the components for chili dogs using the same calculation. The cost of 80% of the $1,000 worth of items, or 16,000 of the 20,000 napkins, would be $800 if they were distributed to customers who purchased chili dogs. It follows that the chili dog line should be associated with $800 of the $1,000 spent on supplies. Can you see how everything comes together? All you're trying to do is connect product lines to running costs, sometimes known as overhead costs. If the $4,000 cost of compensation works similarly, I wouldn't be shocked. But before I continue, I need to clarify a few ABC terminologies. Let's say that all four thousand dollars is used to buy hot dogs for people. **Furthermore, let's assume that there are two steps involved in the standard process for giving a client a hot dog:**

- Grab a hot dog bun.
- The grill should be hot when the frankfurter comes out. Place it in the bun.

On the other hand, serving a chili dog involves five steps:

- Purchase a hot dog bun.
- The grill should be hot when the frankfurter comes out. Place it in the bun.
- Fill the bun with a generous amount of chili.
- Top the bun with an additional generous spoonful of chili.
- Fill the bread with around a third of a spoonful of chili.

(You did really read it accurately.) I believe you can see where this is going. I accomplished something very amazing for a customer, and my business school teachers praised it with a lot of flowery words. In this case, I would contend that the funds are used for what is often called helping others. Here, I should also point out that serving a chili dog customer involves five steps, while serving a typical hot dog customer just requires two. This set of activities is a cost driver. I'm not sure why, but you may not get the idea right away. However, it is common sense to take financial considerations into account. The phrase "cost drivers" only describes the reality that an employee's effort to please a customer is a good indication of their pay. Even if you may already be aware, I will tell you anyway: We can tie the pay cost to each of the regular hot dog and chili dog product lines by counting the steps required to provide them. The total number of steps needed to sell two thousand regular hot dogs is four thousand, as each hot dog takes two steps. If you sell 2,000 chili dogs and make them all in five steps, the queue will have 10,000 steps. By comparing the number of steps in the regular hot dog line to the number of steps in the chili dog line, you can split up the compensation.

You may get a sense of how much of the overall cost goes into making standard hot dogs by using the following calculations:

$4,000 × 14,000 (total steps) / 4,000 (steps for a typical hot dog)

$1,143 is the outcome of this calculation. The cost of pay for each of the chili dog elements may also be allocated using the information in the phases. The potential computation would resemble this: 10,000 steps for chili dogs divided by 14,000 steps for the total is $4,000

This calculation yields $2,857 as the outcome.

Putting in place a basic ABC scheme

+ **Examine your overhead expenses:** Check to see whether there is enough overhead to worry you. ABC may not be the ideal option if your business has high profit margins and minimal operational expenses. Instead of increasing value via more accurate overhead allocation, improper budgeting may be the outcome of an OCD disease.

+ **Determine the high overhead expenses:** If you want to use the ABC strategy to divide your overhead costs, this is a requirement. Avoid wasting time trying to split little amounts unless they are similarly easy to divide and can be completed in parallel with the main activity. If at all feasible, get the most value for your money. Using an ABC strategy, you may easily split off a significant amount of your overhead. Go ahead and be forgiving.

+ **Identify the main operations that use the overhead expenses:** At the fictitious hot dog store, your only duty is to serve customers. That's only the start of what you may hope to achieve. You don't have to write a comprehensive list of 80 things to do, however. Determine your primary responsibilities to cut down your overhead. It will be much simpler to create a budget if you can streamline this procedure. By taking a few steps, you may figure out how to divide the overhead costs across the product lines in a fair and acceptable manner. It is, therefore, the general perspective.

+ **Use the proper measures to track the actions to goods:** Once you understand the simple steps that enable you to relate the overhead expenditures to the product or service lines, be sure to use the appropriate measure, sometimes referred to as a cost driver. Even in the absence of a cost driver, one expenditure in operating the hot dog stand company may be seen as an overhead charge. Was it the cost of rent? Additionally, because the cost of the goods could be viewed at a glance, a cost driver was not required. For the pay cost, a more complex textbook allocation system was required. After that, the price of an activity you came up with called "serving the customer" was divided by the number of steps each product line needed.

Observing how ABC is supported by QuickBooks

+ **Itemized Transactions:** By itemizing transactions in QuickBooks, you may allocate costs to certain tasks or initiatives. Finding out which jobs are expensive and how those costs are distributed may be made easier with this level of information.

+ **Class Tracking:** You may group transactions into many groups or departments using QuickBooks' Class Tracking feature. If you use them to represent various processes inside your firm, it will be easier to evaluate the costs related to each class.

+ **Job Costing:** QuickBooks' job costing tool is useful for companies that need to monitor costs associated with specific projects or client tasks. By utilizing this tool to allocate expenses and income to each activity, you can evaluate how lucrative each one is.

+ **Expense Allocation:** Utilize QuickBooks' expense allocation feature to split up overhead costs across many departments or activities. This helps to better portray the true cost of each activity by connecting indirect expenses to specific actions.

+ **Custom Reports:** You may create custom reports using QuickBooks that are ideal for your business. You may use filters, classifications, and other criteria to break down and analyze costs associated with specific actions that your business does in order to generate activity-based cost reports.

Activating the class tracking system

+ **Select Preferences under Edit:** You can see the Preferences window box in QuickBooks.

+ **Inform QuickBooks that you want to modify the accounting settings:** To access QuickBooks' accounting settings, click the Accounting button in the list box on the left side of the Preferences dialog box and choose the setting you want to change. In this case, you want to change Class Tracking. If you want to change the budgeting process, the Company Preferences page is shown below. Simply click on the name of the Company Preferences tab if you don't see it.

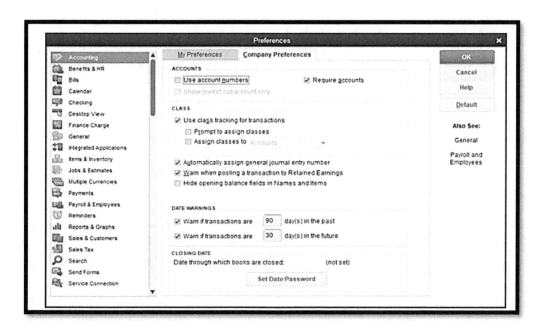

+ To activate class tracking, choose Use Class Tracking for Transactions.
+ As an alternative, you may click the box next to "Prompt to Assign Classes" to tell QuickBooks to use the classes.
+ Next, press the OK button.

This will add a Class drop-down list or field to the Create Invoices, Write Checks, Enter Bills, and any other windows you use to keep track of your income and expenses. Just mark any purchase as being in a certain class.

CHAPTER TEN

CONFIGURATION OF A SYSTEM FOR PROJECT AND JOB COSTING

Configuring a QuickBooks job

Choose "Add Job" from the fast menu by right-clicking on the client you want to choose. Once this step is finished, QuickBooks will show you the New Job window.

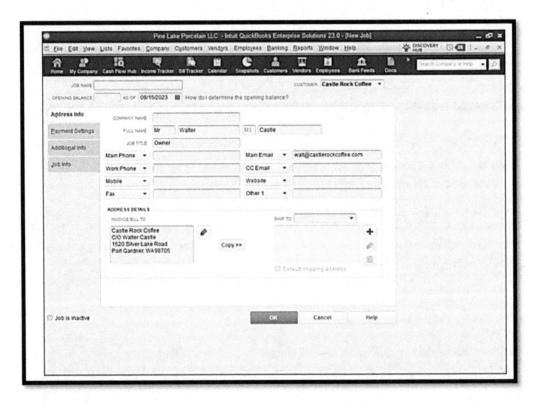

Make sure to provide a name in the "Job Name" field if you are setting up a project or piece of work for a client. Home builders are able to use the house's title as the job since they build houses. Maybe the street address will do. Through the "Address Info," "Payment Settings," "Additional Info," and "Job Info" pages, you may provide additional employment-related information if you'd like. Below is a link to the "Job Info" area on the new job's website. You may find drop-down choices on this page to help you find the state and sort of job you're searching for. In the text fields on the tab, you may additionally enter the work's start date, estimated finish date, and actual end date. The Job Is Inactive checkbox may also be used to hide a job from the list that shows in the Customer Center window when it is no longer in use.

Monitoring the expense of a project or task

You can keep an eye on the revenue and costs related to a task after you add it to the Customer:job list. It is necessary to provide both the job name and the customer in the text box marked "Customer:Job." For example, the following picture shows the Create Invoices window. It is important to note that the "Customer:Job" drop-down option may show both the work name and the customer name. To execute a payment connection linked to a job, you must find the client and the work using the client:job list. That's the only thing needed.

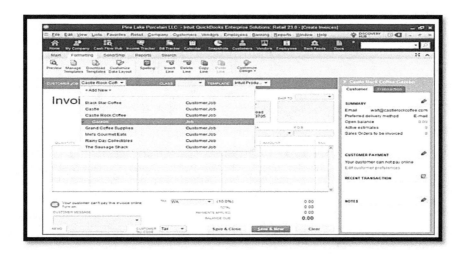

Drop-down lists, also known as Customer:Job and present in other apps, may also be used to track your earnings and expenses. The "Customer:Job" drop-down option that is connected to QuickBooks allows you to note how much time you have spent working on a certain customer's project or assignment. You may examine this data in the "Time/Enter Single Activity" section. To keep track of how much time has been spent on a project, you only need to choose the user and the work using the drop-down list. This is something you should review again.

Reporting job costing

Making use of job estimates

You must first choose the Customers > Create Estimates command in order to produce a task estimate. The "Create Estimates" window appears inside QuickBooks. Within the "Create Invoices" window, you will find instructions on how to complete the boxes in this window. As a general rule, the Create Estimates window is used similarly to the Create Invoices window. It makes sense. In a nutshell, an estimate is only a forecast or illustration of the final cost of a project. It is expected that you will provide the same data and complete the forms in the same way.

In the unlikely event that you did not enable quotations during the original setup of QuickBooks, you may do it later. After choosing the Edit > Preferences command with the keyboard, click the Jobs & Estimates icon that appears in the Preferences window. Next, choose the "Yes" radio button for the option next to the "Company Preferences" tab. You are able to provide estimates, correct? Additionally, if you progress bill, you might think about clicking the "Yes" radio option under the "Do You Do."

Billing progress

In this case, a client will get a charge from you for a part of the entire amount you had previously estimated. Examine the box that says "Create Estimates." Consider that this window is showing a quotation that a customer has asked you to provide them. Additionally, let's suppose for the sake of this discussion that the quote relates to a project you are presently working on as a consultant. The "Create Invoice" button is located at the very top of the Create Estimates box. In order to charge the coaching client for the job later, you will need to click it. If you have already chosen to utilize the progress billing method, QuickBooks will display the window box that lets you construct a progress invoice based on an estimate. Using the facts in the estimate, you may create a statement using this box.

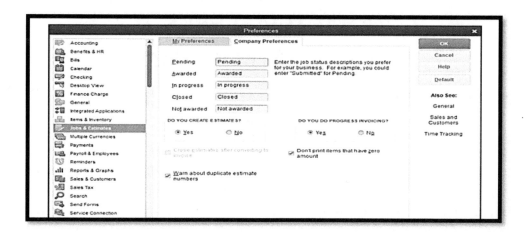

QuickBooks will produce a single invoice that includes all of the data entered in the Create Estimates box if you choose to Create Invoice for the Entire Estimate (100%). You may also choose to just charge a part of the estimate by choosing one of the other options. Using the given radio option, an invoice may be generated for a certain percentage of the entire estimate. After that, you may enter the amount in the "% of Estimate" box. In this case, QuickBooks charges the customer a fee equal to a preset percentage of the estimate. You may also use the radio box labeled "Create Invoice for Selected Items or Different Percentages of Each Item." After this is finished, QuickBooks will let you choose which parts of the goods included in the estimate need to be paid. When you click OK, QuickBooks either shows the Specify Invoice Amounts for Items on Estimate dialog box or creates the invoice using the estimated data. This is due to the fact that you said that you wanted to designate distinct percentages for every item on the invoice. You may choose the anticipated fee you want to charge for the progress report in the Amount section.

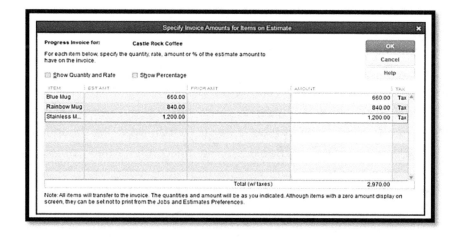

CHAPTER ELEVEN
ANALYSIS OF RATIOS
Disclosing a Few Warnings Regarding Ratio Analysis

An established financial tool called ratio analysis is used by organizations to assess their performance and make wise choices. QuickBooks, one of the most popular accounting programs, makes it easy to generate financial records and key performance indicators that may be used in ratio analysis. **Despite the usefulness of ratio analysis, a few things must be considered to ensure that the results are properly interpreted and that decisions are made.**

- **Data Integrity and Accuracy:** Ensuring that the data submitted into QuickBooks is correct and comprehensive is crucial. Financial data may become distorted if any mistakes or inaccurate information is recorded, which might provide a false impression of a company's true financial condition. To ensure that the findings are accurate, the data must be regularly checked and reviewed.

- **Internal comparisons:** Ratios are most useful when compared to standards that are thought to be inside the same company. The inability of QuickBooks to provide industry-specific criteria, however, makes it difficult to assess a ratio's favorability using this program. To make more accurate comparisons, users can look for corporate information from other sources.

- **Limited Historical Data:** Because of the potential for limited historical data, QuickBooks may not provide you a thorough historical view on financial facts. This limitation makes it more difficult to identify long-term patterns. To get a more complete picture of the past, users may need to export data to other programs or files.

- **Non-Financial Factors:** Although ratio analysis primarily concentrates on financial metrics, it ignores non-financial factors that could affect a company. In order to get a complete picture of the business environment, it is essential to incorporate not only ratio analysis but also elements like shifting market trends, legal and regulatory requirements, or consumer behavior.

- **Inconsistent Accounting Methods:** Because various businesses may use different accounting practices, it might be difficult to compare the financial transaction data. People who use QuickBooks should be careful when comparing numbers with companies that utilize different financial standards or techniques since doing so might lead to inaccurate conclusions.

- **Lack of Context:** Although ratios are helpful, they don't provide the information they display any context. Prior to doing ratio analysis, users should learn a great deal about the company, the sector it works in, and the economy as a whole. They will be able to make well-informed judgments based on the big picture thanks to this.
- **Seasonal variations:** QuickBooks may not be able to appropriately represent changes in financial data depending on the time of year. Enterprises may be significantly impacted by seasonality, and these enterprises may undergo changes that affect their prices differently at various times of the year. It is important for users to understand these differences and modify their research accordingly.
- **Ignoring Qualitative Aspects:** Ratio analysis is a statistical method that may not be able to gauge a company's qualitative attributes, such management caliber, brand perception, or creative ideas. Ratio analysis makes the assumption that quantitative elements are more significant than qualitative ones, which explains this. Customers should combine qualitative and ratio feedback to conduct a more thorough assessment.
- **Debt and Financial Leverage:** QuickBooks may show how much debt a business has taken on overall, but it might not provide a detailed explanation of the conditions and terms of that loan. To have a thorough grasp of how debt affects financial data, users must look into loan agreements, interest rates, and termination dates.
- **Not Considering Future Predictions:** QuickBooks is mostly focused on historical data, which is necessary for assessing prior successes but does not support forecasting. To find possible trends and problems, users are advised to employ projection tools in addition to ratio analysis.

Examining liquidity ratios

A complex picture of a company's ability to satisfy its short-term financial commitments is revealed when its liquidity ratios are seen through the prism of the financial data accessible in QuickBooks. A thorough understanding of a company's cash flow is provided by liquidity metrics, which are crucial to the study of finance because they show how easily a business can turn its assets into cash when needed. The current ratio is one of the most intriguing metrics in QuickBooks. This ratio, which is based on the connection between the company's current assets and current liabilities, may be used to calculate a company's short-term liquidity. By using QuickBooks, accountants may rapidly find out how well a firm can meet its short-term financial responsibilities. The fast ratio, often referred to as the acid-test ratio, allows for an improvement in this assessment. Only the assets with the greatest liquidity are the subject of this ratio. QuickBooks makes it easy to look more closely at cash, stocks that are for sale and accounts that are due for outstanding bills. Removing assets and doing a more comprehensive assessment of the company's liquidity gives a more accurate picture of the current state of the business's finances.

One simple measure that may be readily retrieved from the information kept in QuickBooks is operating cash flow. It is used to assess the liquidity ratio related to the organization's primary operations. One way to gauge how well a business can create cash within its operations is to look at the ratio of its operational cash flow to its current bills. Long-term trends provide a multitude of insights on the changing patterns of liquidity. The cash ratio, which can be found, using QuickBooks data, is one of the most notable liquidity metrics. This ratio shows how much cash and cash equivalents the business has on hand in relation to its current expenses. It gives a precise picture of the resources that the company has at its disposal. Extremely high or low readings may not necessarily imply a desirable liquidity status in every situation, thus it is crucial to assess cash ratios carefully. When it comes to working capital management, QuickBooks is unique in that it makes it possible to keep an eye on crucial elements including suppliers, accounts payable, and accounts outstanding. A precise balance between these elements is necessary to preserve a certain amount of liquidity. Two of the most crucial elements in acquiring strategic leverage are figuring out how to improve working capital cycles and being able to identify trends. Customers may examine receivables turnover in addition to the conventional liquidity measures using accounting software such as QuickBooks. Despite not being a common indicator of liquidity, this provides insight into how quickly a company collects its accounts receivable. The overall financial condition benefits from a higher turnover ratio, which shows that cash is being exchanged efficiently.

It is possible to assess the debt service reimbursement ratio since QuickBooks keeps very accurate records of all debt and interest payments. This measure, which considers both cash flow and debt promises, may be used to assess a company's level of financial stability and its ability to handle its debt commitments, which is a crucial aspect of liquidity. How long it has been since the payables were produced is one of the most crucial items to monitor in QuickBooks. People have access to the bills that the company must pay and the way it handles its payables. Making on-time payments to suppliers is essential for keeping good connections with them and raising the possibility that the company will be able to negotiate better conditions for payments. Although the measures of internal financial ratios are the main focus of the investigation, it is not over yet. The dated debts are an integral part of the story, despite not being a ratio. Tracking how long invoices have been past due is one of the most crucial strategic concerns in QuickBooks. This shows how well lending terms and collection procedures are working, which affects the liquidity fabric as a whole. However, a thorough examination of QuickBooks' liquidity levels may not be limited to only interpreting numerical figures. The context around the data is just as important as the actual figures. It is necessary for users to go beyond the statistics and absorb broader information such as external influences, historical trends, and organizational standards. In order to maintain long-term financial health, it is crucial to be cautious and have backup plans since unforeseen events and changes in the economy may have a big effect on liquidity. In the end, looking at the liquidity levels via the prism of QuickBooks is like to reading a long, detailed story. The story of QuickBooks' data is deeply entwined with the company's capacity to adjust to shifting financial conditions. When data is properly interpreted, it becomes more than just a set of statistics; it becomes a story that helps you make choices and determines how financially stable a company will be in the years to come.

Examining leverage ratios

To successfully navigate the complex world of leverage ratios that exists inside the vast universe of financial data that is included within programs like QuickBooks, one must have a general understanding of what leverage ratios represent as well as the formulae that show how they function with numbers. **These equations, which are kept in the QuickBooks environment, which places a strong focus on data, provide the mathematical basis of a business's financial structure and debt management capabilities.**

   + **Debt-to-Equity Ratio:** This important metric establishes the connection between a company's total debt and the equity held by its owners. **The debt-to-equity ratio is computed as follows: long-term debt divided by shareholders' equity**

One may easily ascertain the owners' entire debt and equity holdings thanks to QuickBooks' database of financial data. This gives you a thorough understanding of the percentage of the company that is financed by debt as opposed to equity.

   + **Interest Coverage Ratio:** Also known as the interest coverage ratio, this ratio shows how well a company can meet its interest obligations. **Interest Coverage Ratio = Operating Income/Interest Expenses is the formula used to calculate it.**

Both labor revenue and interest expenses are easily visible to users of QuickBooks. Considering this, it is evident that the company can handle its interest payments.

   + **Debt Service Coverage Ratio:** The Company's cash flow and loan obligations must be added together before you can determine the debt service coverage ratio. **Debt Service Coverage Ratio = Operating Cash Flow/Debt Obligations is the formula used to calculate it.**

Customers may use QuickBooks to ascertain their continuing cash flow and debt-related responsibilities. Customers are given a real-time picture of the company's ability to meet its financial commitments based on the cash flows produced by its activities.

- The **Equity Ratio** is a metric that shows what percentage of an organization's assets are financed by equity. **The formula is simple to comprehend and straightforward:**

Total Equity/Total Assets equals Equity Ratio

QuickBooks users may easily have a better grasp of the financial situation of their business by seeing the whole stock and total assets of the organization.

- **Ratio of Debt:** One metric that shows the percentage of an asset's value that comes from debt is the Rate of Debt. **The following is the formula's calculation:**

Total Assets/Total Debt equal Debt Ratio

QuickBooks has the capacity to collect financial information and gives users the opportunity to analyze the fine line that separates seizing expansion possibilities from the risks associated with relying too much on loan financing. Users must have a firm grasp of the relevance of these ratios for industry norms, historical trends, and the overall state of the economy in order to properly traverse the complicated numbers provided in these QuickBooks calculations. These percentages are more than just figures; they are part of a financial story that helps people understand the complex relationship between borrowing money and having the ability to pay it back. One way to conceptualize QuickBooks is as a story that tells the story of a business's financial system.

Examining activity ratios

Looking at activity rates through the prism of financial data in software like QuickBooks may provide a story full of efficiency and operational dynamics. Activity ratios, also known as efficiency ratios, may be used to assess a company's capacity to efficiently manage its resources, utilize its assets, and transform inputs into outputs. **These metrics, which are obtained from the complex data included in QuickBooks, provide information on how well a business runs and utilizes its available resources.**

- **Inventory Turnover Ratio:** This ratio shows how successfully a company manages its stock by showing how often it is sold and then refilled over a certain time frame. **Inventory Turnover Ratio is computed as follows: Cost of Goods Sold (COGS)/Average Inventory**

Users may assess the pace at which the company is releasing its items into the market by using QuickBooks, which offers the necessary data points in an understandable style.

- The second metric is the **accounts receivable turnover ratio**, which shows how well the credit and recovery procedures are working. Accounts Receivable Turnover Ratio is computed as follows: Net Credit Sales/Average Accounts Receivable

QuickBooks makes it easier to compute average accounts due and net credit sales, giving a clear picture of how quickly the business settles its debts.

- The **third statistic is the total asset turnover ratio**, which shows how well a business uses its assets to produce income. **The formula is defined as follows in this way:**

Net Sales / Average Total Assets = Total Asset Turnover Ratio

Information regarding the company's net sales and average total assets may be easily obtained using QuickBooks, giving insight into how the firm uses its assets generally.

- **Accounts Payable Turnover Ratio:** This figure shows how rapidly a business reimburses its suppliers. **Accounts Payable Turnover Ratio is computed as follows: Net Credit Purchases/Average Accounts Net credit sales and average accounts** due may be easily calculated using payable accounting software like QuickBooks, leading to more efficient payables management.
- **Fixed Asset Turnover Ratio:** This statistic is used to assess how well a business exploits its fixed assets to produce revenue. **Fixed Asset Turnover Ratio = Net Sales/Average Fixed Assets** is the formula used to compute it.

Net sales and average fixed assets are useful metrics that show how well fixed assets are being used, and QuickBooks is a useful tool for obtaining this data.

- The **Cash Conversion Cycle** is a process that shows how long it takes a business to turn the money it spends on resources and commodities into cash flows. **Despite not being a traditional ratio, the formula consists of three main parts:**

Days Inventory Outstanding (DIO) + Days Sales Outstanding (DSO) − Days Payables Outstanding (DPO) = Cash Conversion Cycle

Customers that use QuickBooks can keep an eye on DIO, DSO, and DPO, giving them a thorough understanding of the organization's cash flow. When people look at these activity rates using QuickBooks, the numbers become scenes in a story that shows how successfully a company runs its operations and manages its resources. Apart from the technique, it is crucial to have a firm grasp of this data in relation to industry-specific business environment elements, historical patterns, and standards in the same sector. QuickBooks acts as a watchdog and an explainer, giving people a glimpse of how a business functions and helping them understand the complex, multidimensional structure of the activity levels it encounters.

Examining profitability ratios

Analyzing the success rates found in the enormous volumes of financial data that are available via programs like QuickBooks may provide an intriguing story about a company's ability to create value and make money. Profitability metrics are a kind of guide that helps people understand how effectively and efficiently a business turns its inputs into cash. **These percentages are converted into numerical figures when utilized** with QuickBooks, which show how financially, successful a business is and how long it will continue to grow:

- Net Profit Margin: One of the most important indicators of a company's profitability. It shows the percentage of revenue that is left over as profit after all costs have been subtracted. This is a succinct method.

Net Profit/Net Sales = Net Profit Margin

QuickBooks becomes a platform that lets users easily see their net profit and net sales, giving them a clear picture of how well the business can turn sales into profits.

- Gross Profit Margin: After subtracting the cost of the sold goods, the gross profit margin is the portion of the total sales price that the business kept. The following is how the code is written:

Gross Profit/Net Sales = Gross Profit Margin

You can quickly access the gross profit and net sales statistics by using QuickBooks, which gives you information on how well your pricing and production methods are working.

- Return on Assets (ROA): An organization's ability to make money off of its assets is gauged by the return on assets (ROA) ratio. The code describing this ratio is as follows:

Net Profit divided by Average Total Assets is ROA.

Calculating the company's net profit and average total assets is made easy using QuickBooks. This gives information on the company's ability to make money off of its assets.

- ROE, or return on equity: It makes use of the Return on Equity (ROE) ratio. For the purpose of figuring out the owners' stock value. ROE=Net Profit/Average Shareholders' Equity provides the solution.

One useful tool for figuring out a company's net profit and average owners' equity is QuickBooks. This data shows how well the business makes use of equity to produce income.

- Operating Profit Margin: This metric, which gauges the profitability of the company's basic activities, does not account for taxes or interest. The process is quick:

Operating Profit/Net Sales = Operating Profit Margin

Running profit and net sales may be easily calculated using QuickBooks, giving you a clear view of how successful your company operations are.

- Earnings per Share (EPS): This number shows how much money each share of stock is now worth. It is simple to understand the process:

The ratio of net profit to outstanding shares is known as EPS

Users of QuickBooks, a database of financial data, may get information on the number of active shares and net profit, which in turn gives them insight into the distribution of the company's profits. When people use QuickBooks to look into these success rates, the numbers become scenes in a story that shows how profitable a business is and how much money it can make. Being both a writer and a collection of data, QuickBooks serves as the foundation for the revenue narrative, helping everyone involved comprehend the nuances of a business's financial performance. Along with the techniques, it is crucial to fully comprehend these figures in light of industry norms, past patterns, and the particulars of the company sector.

CHAPTER TWELVE
ANALYSIS OF AN ECONOMIC VALUE ADDED (EVA)

Presenting the EVA Logic

The general idea known as the Logic of Economic Value Added (EVA) has become well-liked in the domains of financial analysis and corporate performance evaluation. Stewart Stern created the intricate EVA metric in the latter half of the 20th century to assess a company's true economic return while accounting for the cost of capital. While net operating profit after taxes (NOPAT) and profits before interest and taxes (EVA) are similar concepts, EVA varies in that it considers the cost of capital as a substantial component. The core tenet of EVA is that a business should make more money than it spends on capital expenditures. By deducting the cost of capital from operational profit, EVA aims to ascertain the extra value that a company creates. By deducting the company's cost of capital from its net operating profit after taxes, you may determine EVA. Both the cost of loans and the cost of shares are included in the cost of capital, often known as the weighted average cost of capital (WACC). By accounting for the possible cost of deploying capital, this comprehensive approach to income assessment aims to provide a more realistic picture of a business's financial performance. The foundation of EVA is the idea that managers need to choose actions that optimize shareholder value. It asserts that a business must continuously generate profits greater than the cost of the capital it has invested in order to turn a profit. The EVA assessment, which offers a more complete picture than just financial performance, includes the cost of capital. One of the finest features of EVA is its ability to monitor both financial and operational performance in one place. By examining how the income statement and balance sheet evolve over time, it shows the overall picture and closes the gap between accounting and finance. Because it employs an integrated approach, EVA is a potent tool for assessing a company's true economic health.

By motivating managers to concentrate on generating long-term value, EVA not only measures the past but also predicts the future. By aligning managers' and owners' objectives, an emphasis on economic profit promotes a long-term strategic mindset that transcends immediate financial advantages. The goal of EVA is to illustrate future developments. Proponents of EVA contend that there are many more benefits to using it as a performance evaluation tool than drawbacks. This is despite the fact that some people think that using EVA might be difficult since calculating the cost of capital is a subjective process and financial data can be manipulated. For instance: I'll give you a mathematical example to show you why this is true. Assume that after you pay yourself a fair wage, your business generates an extra $20,000. Furthermore, suppose you get the chance to sell your business to a rival for $200,000, put the money you receive in a stock mutual fund, and earn around $20,000 annually. (I understand that neither your company nor the stock market can provide returns of 10% annually. Let's suppose that these figures are correct for the sake of this discussion.) You do get paid, yes. Naturally, you and your family are receiving compensation for the money they invested. But that's all you're receiving. You may as well sell your firm, reinvest the proceeds in the stock market (as one possibility), and take a position with the telephone company if you wish to acquire anything else. It is not a smart idea to operate your own firm in this straightforward situation. I'm not attempting to persuade you to sell your business, so please don't be upset with me. Rather, I will show you how to more effectively manage your business by using EVA, a very effective tool.

Observing EVA in operation

EVA analysis comes in two varieties. I'll begin with the simplest. If I start with the basic form, you may be able to grasp all the little features of the EVA model from the outset. After completing the simpler kind of EVA study, known as equity-based EVA, you may proceed to the more complex EVA model. I want you to look at a couple bank accounts before I continue our conversation. A simple income statement and balance sheet are shown in the first and second images, respectively. Much of the information you need to do an EVA analysis for your business may be found in these two financial records. Assume that these two financial documents accurately reflect the nature of your business.

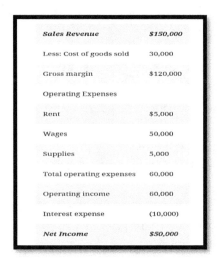

Sales Revenue	$150,000
Less: Cost of goods sold	30,000
Gross margin	$120,000
Operating Expenses	
Rent	$5,000
Wages	50,000
Supplies	5,000
Total operating expenses	60,000
Operating income	60,000
Interest expense	(10,000)
Net Income	$50,000

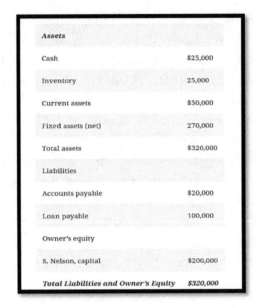

Assets	
Cash	$25,000
Inventory	25,000
Current assets	$50,000
Fixed assets (net)	270,000
Total assets	$320,000
Liabilities	
Accounts payable	$20,000
Loan payable	100,000
Owner's equity	
S. Nelson, capital	$200,000
Total Liabilities and Owner's Equity	*$320,000*

An EVA figure that is positive means that your company is profitable. This shows that the company has some money left over after paying employees' salary, loan interest, and owner returns. The benefit of having additional funding is that it enables the company to turn a profit. In essence, EVA charges for the cash you have invested in a firm. To find out whether you are profitable, you deduct this expense from your net income. The cost of the capital multiplied by the total quantity of capital invested throughout the business period is the capital charge. Typically, the cost of capital is expressed as an annual return percentage or an interest rate. Your business's invested capital is equivalent to your owner's stock. The return on the cost of capital is equivalent to the return on an equally risky investment in anything else.

An illustration of EVA

Using the data from the first and second images, the following formula may be used to determine each of these amounts:

- Determine the capital charge: Consider, for example, the situation where you invest money in the company that is shown in the pictures and get a twenty percent return on your investment.

In this case, an EVA may be computed using the following method: 20% × $200,000 (of owner's equity) is the capital charge.

The only shareholder in a small business run and owned by an entrepreneur is the owner/entrepreneur. The sum that should be given back to the owners is $40,000, which is the capital charge that this method gives us.

✦ **Take the net income and subtract the capital charge:** Applying the above process will enable you to determine the EVA. In the first example, the net income is $50,000.

EVA is equal to net income ($50,000) minus capital charge ($40,000).

It is the result that equals the $10,000 EVA. Therefore, you will discover that this business is profitable if you use the information from the firm that is shown in the photos and estimate that the cost of capital is twenty percent. The business has ten thousand dollars left over after paying everyone their fair share, which is known as an economic profit.

Another illustration of EVA

Let's say that the actual capital charge is $50,000 in order to get on with this scenario. This may be calculated by multiplying the owner's stock or capital of $200,000 by a 25% cost of capital figure. In this case, what does the EVA mean? This question has no solution. This means that the business does not produce any EVA if it earns a $50,000 profit but the investors demand a $50,000 return (which can be calculated by multiplying 25% by $200,000). Is the scenario outlined above something you can understand? You shouldn't get too engrossed in the calculations, even if the figures could seem overwhelming. I think you understand the general functions of EVA analysis. If you owned a business like the one in the pictures, you would expect to get a good return on the capital you and your family had put into it. You are not progressing, however, if you are just earning the same amount of money that you might in another venture, like a stock mutual fund. If everything went as planned, EVA research would ensure that you would obtain a return on your investment that was more than sufficient. That's the only thing it does.

Reviewing a Few Crucial EVA Points

When doing an EVA study, your goal is simple: you want to find out whether running your business is making money for you.

Generally speaking, you should think about a few things to make sure your study is headed in the right direction:

✦ **What is the quality of the numbers?** This is a critical point. Does the amount you produced (one of the figures you used) and the amount you may be able to sell it for and then reinvest (another crucial number you used) appear on your income statement and balance sheet when you complete your math? Numbers that aren't quite correct will always be a part of your life. It's just the current situation. However, those two figures include several errors that skew the results. **Advice:** In your EVA research, you should utilize the cash-out value rather than the owner's equity value if the two are significantly different. The owner's equity value is the amount that appears on your balance sheet. One useful tip is to figure out how much owner's equity you have and compare it to the amount you think you would get if you sold your company.

+ **To what extent is the cost of capital % favorable?** A significant component of determining the capital charge is the cost of capital worth. It's difficult to come up with this figure, to be honest. Developing a figure for a billion-dollar corporation would likely need a team of PhDs. The tiny company cannot do this. I believe you ought to utilize a collection of integers as a result. Many people believe that a small firm, which is defined as any company with revenues under, say, $50 million, has an annual return of 20% to 25%. It seems like an excellent collection of numbers to utilize for EVA study. The cost of capital rates for large businesses is about 10 to 12 percent, which may also be of interest to you. You would never want to be so low. Also, remember that venture capital returns, which are generated by the most successful and fastest-growing smallest firms, typically range from 35 to 45 percent annually. It would seem that the cost of capital rates you used in your EVA computation need to be far lower than this. For the majority of enterprises, the rate of return on capital should be far lower than 35 to 45 percent. **Advice:** Experimenting with a few different speeds is a smart idea while studying EVA. For example, your cost of capital could start at 15%. You might then go to 20%, 25%, and 30%. The calculation is rather easy if you have the owner's stock number and the return number. Coming up with many values for EVA is not at all difficult.

+ **How does psychological income factor in?** I believe it's OK to add psychological income if the company is owned and operated by only one person. It is impossible to overlook the business. A healthy, successful firm, particularly one that is yours, should eventually earn a profit and pay back the money it borrows. However, I'm not the one who believes you should sell your farm and leave your work at the neighborhood big-box shop if you like what you do. Wearing an orange vest and working on concrete floors all day is perfectly acceptable, in my opinion. My argument is that, in my opinion, running your own company involves more than simply earning money.

+ **Have there been any variations?** Results vary over time in many small companies, including the ones I've owned and operated. This is yet another crucial element. You can't simply decide to quit after one year, even if it's a very horrible one. For the same reason, you shouldn't decide to purchase a property in the south of France based on only one terrible year. An EVA study's sources need to reflect the overall health of the company. For instance, they need to display the overall

97

income level, the total amount that may be cashed out, the estimated general cost of capital, and so on. I don't believe you can rely on the findings of your EVA research if something strange occurs one year and puts one of these sources out of balance.

+ **Is there a unique circumstance facing your company?** It is often known that EVA analysis is a difficult task that may sometimes not be completed at all. For example, many people who are passionate about EVA analysis are eager to point out that new enterprises do not benefit much from an EVA research. This is due to the fact that the income statement does not provide a clear picture of how much value the business is producing. However, it is impossible to ascertain the kind of profit the company has earned because of this ambiguity. It is crucial to remember that this is a circumstance that ought to be comprehensible. It is a given that the company will either lose money or earn very little during the first year or two of operation. This is just OK.

The only factors that count are what you assume and what you include in your EVA calculation. The trend or pattern in EVA values is probably more significant to company owners than a single figure. "Am I making money by running my own business?" is a question you should constantly ask yourself while keeping an eye on the wider picture.

When your Company Has Debt, Use EVA

A slightly more involved EVA model allows you to see this additional curve, and because this is very helpful, I will give you a couple of examples below of how this slightly more complex EVA model works. EVA research becomes challenging to perform on a computer when organizations are very large. I don't go into much detail about probable problems here, but you should already be aware of one common problem, which is debt. As a result, debts like bank loans, credit lines, mortgages, and other types of debt can be restructured to help a business make more money.

The first illustration of the altered EVA formula

If your company is allowed to rearrange its bills, you may want to make the following two changes to the EVA analysis:
+ You may need to use a full cost of capital, which is a metric that accounts for the cost of stock as well as the cost of any potential loans.
+ In order to arrive at an appropriate figure, you must include both the amounts paid to borrowers and shareholders in your net income calculation.

Calculating an all-inclusive cost of capital is the first step. For example, if a business gets its capital from three sources—trade suppliers, a bank that charges 10% interest on loans, and owner stock—the following example shows one way to determine the capital charge that must be compared to the net income after accounting for this additional debt.

Trade Vendors ($20,000 @ 0 Percent)	*$0*
Bank loan ($100,000 @ 10 percent)	10,000
Owner's equity ($200,000 @ 20 percent)	40,000
Adjusted Capital Charge	*$50,000*

Even if the statistics in the third image are rather easy to understand, allow me to explain them:

- **Trade vendors:** As you already pay trade partners for the goods and services they provide, any hidden fees that the company charges them are already deducted, so that part of the capital charge is zero. The second picture shows that trade vendors owe the company a total of $20,000, but the company is not obligated to pay those debtors any money.
- **Bank loan:** A 10% fee is added to this $100,000 bank loan, resulting in a $10,000 capital charge. In other words, the company must pay the bank $10,000 year in order to utilize its capital.
- **Owner's equity:** This is the final component of the capital charge and the amount that the company pays its owners. The capital charge for the owner's stock is $40,000 in the third picture; to calculate this capital price, take the cost of the capital portion (20%) and add it to the owner's share; for instance, 20% of $200,000 is $40,000. This results in a new capital charge of $50,000.

Okay. Things are going well so far. Adding back the interest paid to lenders is the second step in using this slightly more difficult EVA model. This gives you an updated income number. Take a moment to think about this. The company made $50,000 (shown in the first picture), but $10,000 was spent on interest, so this number has already been lowered. Therefore, to compare the money that the company made with the money that can be used to pay back the capital sources, you need to add back the $10,000 in interest costs.

This means that when you add up all of the capital sources of return, such as interest or profits, you get $50,000 in net income in addition to $10,000 in interest costs. Doesn't that make sense? After everything is said and done, there is still money left over to pay out owners and creditors. The first graphic is the income statement, and that pot of money includes both the $10,000 in interest expenses and the $50,000 in net revenue. After obtaining an all-inclusive cost of capital and a decreased revenue amount, you can calculate the EVA conventionally. **In this particular scenario, you will apply the following computation method:**

Weighted cost of capital charge ($50,000) minus adjusted income ($60,000)

$10,000 is the amount that symbolizes the EVA as a consequence.

The fact that the easy and more complex EVA formulas provide the same result is not an error; if both the easy and complex methods are correct, then using the complex formula should not alter the EVA; however, this is not the case, and the more complex method enables you to observe how the EVA changes as your debt does.

Introducing two last pointers

1. Even if you don't study the numbers on the back of an envelope, EVA analysis is a good way to think about how you should run your business and whether it makes sense to make changes. It's a good idea to compare your company's net income to what you could make by selling and then putting the capital into something else. EVA analysis is most helpful as a thinking tool for business owners and managers, or at least for owners and managers of small and medium-sized firms.

"Listen to the universe." My friends who are writing agents often tell me this, and I think it's a very good piece of advice, especially when it comes to the financial aspects of running a business. When you think about your business, you should pay attention to the economy. EVA gives you a way to do that. A business must give something back to everyone who has an interest in it, including paying wages to employees, interest and debt service to lenders, owners who put capital, and hopefully you, the owner. A company must pay more than its capital charge in order to turn a profit.

2. Although EVA analysis can be used to analyze a company as a whole, it can also be used to analyze a specific business sector, a particular product line, your management, and other aspects of your company with a little bit of work.

When you think about it, this is cool. You can use EVA analysis to break down your business into different profit-generating activities, and by looking at the economic profit of these different profit activities, you can probably determine which ones should be prioritized because they generate revenue and which ones might need to be stopped because they don't. You can rate bosses and buyers in the same way. If you want to do this more in-depth EVA study, you should use a chart of accounts that allows you to create more comprehensive balance sheets and income statements. If you want to divide your business into two parts, you should use a chart of accounts that makes it easy to view the income statement for each of the two parts. Similarly, you should use a chart of accounts that allows you to see how much money each business unit has spent on capital.

CHAPTER THIRTEEN
QUICKBOOKS 2025: PRIVACY AND DATA SECURITY

Comprehending Data Security

The data security elements of QuickBooks must be understood by every business that utilizes the program to manage its finances. Here is a thorough explanation of all the many components of QuickBooks' data security, including best practices, built-in tools, and additional considerations to make sure your data is secure.

QuickBooks' Built-In Security Features

1. **Permissions for Users:** By configuring and controlling user rights in QuickBooks, you can ensure that only authorized personnel have access to certain financial data.

QuickBooks Desktop:
- Assign roles with different levels of access.
- Reduce the amount of unapproved access to payroll and financial records.
- Utilize the Audit Trail feature to monitor user activity.

QuickBooks Online:
- Assign users to certain roles, such Reports Only, Standard User, or Admin.
- Ensure that different users have access to different levels.
- To monitor changes made by users, utilize the Activity Log.

2. **Encryption:** Data Encryption and Cryptography QuickBooks uses encryption technology to safeguard your data while it is being sent and stored.

Data Transmission:
- SSL (Secure Sockets Layer) technology encrypts the data as it moves from your browser to QuickBooks servers. Specifically, QuickBooks Online does this.
- QuickBooks Desktop may be configured to use SSL to connect to online services.

Data Storage:
- Industry-leading encryption algorithms are used to encrypt all data stored by QuickBooks Online.
- To protect your company's data in QuickBooks Desktop, you may use a password.

3. **MFA or multi-factor authentication:** When logging into QuickBooks Online, users may use multi-factor authentication (MFA) to demand an additional verification step, such a code sent to their mobile device. Account security is improved by this.

4. **Backups that happen automatically:** QuickBooks offers automatic backup options to ease your concerns about data loss.

Online QuickBooks:
- Regular automated backups ensure that your data is safe and constantly current.

QuickBooks Desktop:
- QuickBooks Desktop offers users the ability to set up local backups automatically.
- QuickBooks Desktop also offers a secure cloud backup option.

QuickBooks Data Security Best Practices

- **Frequent updates to software:** Always keep QuickBooks updated to protect yourself from security vulnerabilities.
  - Verify that QuickBooks Online is configured to update automatically.
  - You should install QuickBooks Desktop updates on a regular basis.
- **Secure Passwords:** Use strong, one-of-a-kind passwords for QuickBooks and change them often.
  - Use capital and lowercase characters, numbers, and symbols.
  - Avoid using commonplace or easily guessed information, such as words or birthdays.
- **Management of Users:** Manage user access effectively to reduce the risk of unauthorized access.
  - Review user permissions often to keep them current.
  - Eliminate previous employees or contractors as quickly as you can.
- **Safe Networks:** Only access your QuickBooks data from secure networks to keep it safe from inquisitive eyes.
  - Avoid utilizing public Wi-Fi while using QuickBooks.
  - Use a virtual private network (VPN) while using QuickBooks remotely.
- **Data Backup:** To guard against hardware failure or other issues, periodically backup your QuickBooks data.
  - Regular backups of QuickBooks Desktop are recommended.
  - You should make use of QuickBooks Online's automatic backup feature.

Extra Security Points to Remember

- **Integrations with Third Parties:** Make sure that any third-party applications you want to connect with QuickBooks follow strict security guidelines.
  - Examine the security policies and practices of the third-party supplier.
  - Limit the permissions and capabilities available to third-party applications.

- Employee Training Educate employees on data security best practices to reduce the possibility of human error-driven data breaches.
  - Training on identifying phishing and other types of cybercrime should be provided.
  - Encourage your employees to report any suspicious activity right away.
- **Safety of the Body:** Protect the hardware and servers that house QuickBooks data.
  - Secure cabinets or rooms are the best places to keep servers and backup equipment.
  - Verify that access restrictions are in place in any physical locations that hold sensitive data.
- **Frequent Examinations:** Regular security audits can help you identify and address security vulnerabilities.
  - Regular reviews of audit trails and user access records are necessary.
  - Regularly do out vulnerability assessments and penetration testing.

QuickBooks Compliance and Security Certifications

- **Compliance with PCI:** QuickBooks is PCI DSS certified if you're seeking for a solution to take credit card payments.
  - Assures the safe handling of financial data.
  - Reduces the possibility of credit card information being compromised.
- **Compliance with SOC 2:** QuickBooks Online conforms with SOC 2 (Service Organization Control 2) standards, which include data security, availability, processing integrity, confidentiality, and privacy.
  - Assures users that QuickBooks complies with the highest data security requirements.
  - Ensures the security of customer information.

Addressing Security-Related Issues

- **Plan for Incident Response:** Be Ready for Anything Unexpected Create a plan to address data loss and security breaches as soon as they happen.
  - In the case of a security breach, determine who is in charge of what.
  - Create procedures for occurrence reduction, containment, and detection.
- **Recovery of Data:** In the case of a security incident or hardware breakdown, be ready to recover QuickBooks data.
  - Always ensure that your recovery and backup processes are adequate.
  - Maintain several backup copies in different locations.

The QuickBooks Data File Backup

Your or a colleague's first priority should be to duplicate the QuickBooks data file. Since the QuickBooks data file is one of the most important things on your hard drive, you should handle it with extreme caution. The QuickBooks data file may tell you all you need to know about the financial health of your business. You should never take the chance of losing the file. You could not be aware of your financial status if you lose the data file. Additionally, your yearly tax returns will be erroneous and time-consuming.

Basics of backing up

Fortunately, creating a backup of the QuickBooks data file is not difficult. There are nine stages to follow:

✦ **Select the command File > Create Copy:** The first box that appears in QuickBooks is for backup or copy saving. You have three choices in this window: make a copy for your accountant, save a backup copy of your QuickBooks file, or make a portable business file.

✦ **To save a copy, choose the Backup Copy option button; to continue, click Next:** When you move the QuickBooks file, you may choose to make a portable business file or a full backup. Due to its bigger size, a backup file is easier to move than a portable business file. For example, it could be easier to provide a portable business file. The problem with portable business files is that QuickBooks has to work hard to make them smaller. QuickBooks will need to do further steps to remove the file's restriction if you want to access it again. You may store a copy or backup in the second box that appears when you click Next. The File > Create Backup menu item provides immediate access to the Save Copy or Backup text box.

⊹ Decide whether you want to save your backup file in QuickBooks' offshore data center or on the PC at your company. By choosing "Local Backup," you are indicating that you want to save a copy of your file on a removable storage device, such a USB external drive, or on the hard disk of your computer.

⊹ Click the "Options" option to choose where to store the backup. You may see the Backup Options window box in QuickBooks.

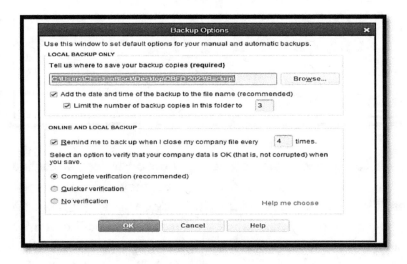

- Select the disk or location where the backed-up corporate file should be stored. In the text box, provide a name to tell QuickBooks where to save your backups. The Browse button may be used if you are not sure how to input a pathname. Using the folder list that shows up in the Browse for Folder box, you can choose which disk or folder to use as a backup in QuickBooks.
- (Alternative) Decide on your backup plans. In the Backup Options dialog box, you can also choose how and when QuickBooks should do backups.
  - Time stamps may be added by using the "Add the Date and Time of the Backup to the File Name (Recommended)" option.
  - **Restricting backup copies:** Simply check the box next to "Limit the Number of Backup Copies in This Folder to X" to tell QuickBooks to remove previous backup copies. Next, enter the number of backup copies you want QuickBooks to retain in the text box next to it.
  - You may set up backup reminders by selecting the "Remind Me to Back Up When I Close My Company File Every X Times" option. This will guarantee that you regularly backup your QuickBooks file everytime you close QuickBooks. A variety of intervals may be chosen, including "every time," "every other time," "every third time," and others.
  - **Turning on data verification:** Indicate to QuickBooks that it should use the verification buttons to confirm the correctness of your data backups. From the drop-down option, choose "Complete Verification (Recommended)" for the most thorough and effective verification in QuickBooks. If you are pressed for time and don't have time to verify your data again, you may use the "Quicker Verification" option. It is advisable to just pick the "No Verification" option and not be cautious at all since being cautious is for kids anyhow.
- Once the backup location and options have been chosen, click OK and then Next. There is an option you may click to find out when QuickBooks will make a backup.
- Choose the time you want to run the backup. The most common choice is to choose Backup from the Save Copy or Backup menu. On the "when" question that QuickBooks asks you, choose "Save It Now" from the "Save Copy or Backup" choice. By choosing "Save It Now and Schedule Future Backups" or "Only Schedule Future Backups" when prompted "when" to do a backup, you may instruct QuickBooks to perform regular data backups. Tell QuickBooks you want to arrange backups, and it will display a few dialog boxes for you to complete the task. This will establish a new backup schedule. The backups may be scheduled to run on certain days and at particular times, and the schedule can be given a name.

- Press "Finish" to close the "Save Copy or Backup" window. Click "Finish" after you're satisfied with the backup's functioning. The current QuickBooks business file is copied and stored somewhere else; this is known as a backup.

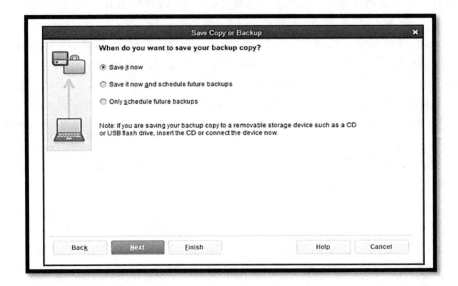

Online backup, what about it?

If you're looking closely, you may have noticed that the Save Copy or Backup text box has an option button for Online Backup. You may learn more about making an online backup of your QuickBooks business file by selecting that option, which will direct you to a website. The backup will be saved on Intuit's computer network rather than on your computer or a portable CD.

I believe you should think about using online backup for two reasons:

- **Reasonable price:** You may opt to back up all of your PC's information or only QuickBooks, and an annual membership will cost more than a monthly one. Online backup is cheap, and if you have QuickBooks Desktop Pro Plus, Premier Plus, or Enterprise, it may even be free. The most economical choice seems to be a yearly contract to backup all of your information.
- **Less work:** If you have a good Internet connection, saving files online may be a more routine and simple process. You won't have to remember where to store the disk and when to make backups.

Before I go, let me say two last things: I do make backups of all of my important data using QuickBooks' online backup function. They don't pay me to promote Intuit's product in a discreet manner. A folder containing backup data may be synchronized with a cloud-based backup service like Google Drive, Dropbox, or OneDrive. Any of these providers may offer you a free cloud backup if you use their free storage space. Simply set it and forget about it. This service may be helpful to those who are living on a tight budget or who don't have a lot of extra money.

A few backup strategies

Reversing is usually the wise course of action. **However, I'll give you some recommendations on when, how, and maybe even why you should backup:**

- Keep it easy. Although I mentioned this in my earlier post on the online backup option, I feel obligated to stress its importance once again. This is the first step in backing up your QuickBooks files: Make backups easier. This implies that utilizing the Internet could be something you want to think about. You will need a portable, high-density storage device that can be connected to the QuickBooks PC, however, if you choose to stay on-site. My preferred gadget is a little USB flash drive. The storage device you choose should be just as easy to use as the one that suits you the best. Right now, "easy" means that it's more likely that you'll turn around.

- Make a backup at all times. It is strongly advised that you make a backup of your data file each time you submit a transaction into QuickBooks. If it takes a lot of work to back up, you generally won't. You should often do backups, provided that you have a handy backup procedure and a location for your backups. It's not extravagant to do it every day.

- Store a backup copy of the QuickBooks file in a different location. Lastly, it's important to remember that a lot of the causes, like a virus, a broken hard drive, human mistake, etc., are unique to your machine and might damage or erase your data files. However, the possibility of specific risks to the integrity or destruction of your QuickBooks file depends on where it is located. Both the QuickBooks file and its backup may be lost in a calamity such a fire, water, or theft. You should thus save a copy of the backup in a different place. Imagine that at the end of the workweek, you can't wait to take the flash drive home. It might fit in your shirt pocket or a handbag. In the event that the QuickBooks data file is altered or deleted take care to ensure that the backup file is not lost along with the original. There are even more reasons to keep your data online.

Restoring a Data File in QuickBooks

You'll need a method to recover the data file so you can resume using QuickBooks if you misplace or destroy the working copy. Restoring the QuickBooks file from a backup is easy. You'll have to start over from scratch if you don't backup the QuickBooks file right away. QuickBooks must be reinstalled, configured, and all of your old data must be entered from scratch. You will have to start again from the beginning if you edit or remove a file without first saving it. You may recover the QuickBooks data file by just inserting the backup disc or USB flash drive into the disk or by downloading the backup file from cloud storage. **Next, follow these steps:**

⤶ Launch QuickBooks and choose the File option. Next, choose Restore Company or Open Company. QuickBooks displays the "Open or Restore Company" dialog box.

⤶ **Be careful to indicate the file type you want to recover:** A typical QuickBooks data file may be opened. QuickBooks may be restored from a portable version or a backup copy. A copy transfer file that an accountant uses may be changed. As one would expect, all you have to do to restore a backup copy is click the "Restore a Backup Copy" option button.

⤶ **Click "Next."** Below is a modified version of the Open or Restore Company text box in QuickBooks.

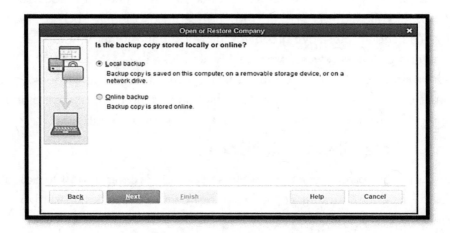

- **Tell QuickBooks whether the backup copy is kept at your company or at an overseas data center:** To do this, choose the "Where is my backup copy file?" option.
- **Click "Next."** QuickBooks displays the "Open Backup Copy" dialog box.

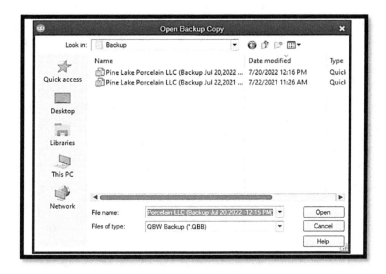

- **Select the backup file you want to use for the restoration, then double-click or select "Open."** Just provide the backup file's location and give it a name that will be used throughout the recovery. Use the Look In drop-down option to find the backup file's location.
- **Select "Open."** QuickBooks displays an alternate version of the Open or Restore Company dialog box, but it is invisible. This only lets you know that a popup to choose the location for the restored file will appear soon. Something doesn't seem right: When QuickBooks is ready to make an inquiry, you should be informed beforehand. But we'll refrain from talking about it. You must delete the current file version in order to recover the firm data file from a backup copy. You may also assert that QuickBooks will just transfer the backup file and replace the original when you need to recover data from a company file. Before trying to restore corporate data files, be sure you have the right backup copy and have overwritten the faulty business file you need to restore. You may choose to rename the recovered file if you would rather not delete or replace the old (possibly damaged) QuickBooks data file. This is what you'll do in Step 9.
- **Click the Next icon:** QuickBooks displays the Save Company File As text box.
- **Allow QuickBooks to locate the backup copy, then choose "Save."** In the store Company File As box, choose where to store the backup file. Most likely, you'll

choose the same place as the last file. If you use the same name for both files in this scenario, QuickBooks will ask you to confirm that you want to replace the old file with the new one. Press "Yes." QuickBooks will provide a new dialog box called Delete Entire File. Enter "yes" in the dialog box to acknowledge deleting the current (and probably corrupt) corporate data file. Then click OK. The backup copy is written over the company file when QuickBooks wishes to restore it. But keep in mind that you might choose a different name for the recovered file. The obnoxious dialog boxes are no longer present. Oh my god.

Just so you know, if you restore your data file to a version that is more current than the one you used to generate the backups, QuickBooks will request your consent to update the business file to the new version. To check the box, just say, "Hey, man, I understand that my company file will be updated to the new version."

⬥ **Add any transactions that have occurred since the previous backup:** During the previous backup, transactions were added to your QuickBooks business file. You'll have to enter those transactions again. For instance, you will need to enter all of your activities from the QuickBooks backup from last Friday once again.

Simplifying the files for QuickBooks Company

The practice of condensing a QuickBooks file has two purposes: The QuickBooks Condense order generates a copy of the QuickBooks data file that is always valid. (We refer to this backup copy as an archive copy.) A corporate file archive copy is similar to a snapshot of the file at a certain point in time. The archived copy of the data file may be used to search for the corporate file if someone has a question about it later. Such a person may be an accountant or a federal or state auditor. The file condensing technique reduces the size of the data file by combining a number of previously closed, in-depth transactions that make use of monster journal entries. I'll provide a quick rundown of what happens when you compress the QuickBooks company file since it might be difficult to keep track of all this saving and condensing. **Throughout the procedure, QuickBooks will usually do the following:**

⬥ Preserves a backup copy of your business's documents: When you minimize the QuickBooks business file, an archived version of your company's files is kept.
⬥ Eliminates closed deals: QuickBooks lets you delete closed transactions from the current version of your business file as part of its consolidation process. Keep in mind that you make an unbreakable duplicate of your QuickBooks business file when you save. You may still view the working version of the QuickBooks company file, however. Outdated, stalled transactions are eliminated from this current, working edition of QuickBooks in order to clean up the company file. QuickBooks no longer needs to keep thorough records of completed transactions.

After payment is received, a transaction is no longer considered an unpaid customer bill. As soon as the seller gets the cleared check from your bank, the deal is complete.

- Provides a summary of completed transactions: Since the closed transactions are removed from the QuickBooks data file, condensing usually creates monthly journal entries that describe the new open transactions that replace the previous closed ones. The recently generated open transactions are then included into the QuickBooks data file that is now active. After you have finished these monthly summary diary entries, you may go on to creating monthly cash accounts. You may still construct financial records for January 2021 in 2024, even when archiving eliminates all the old, suspended agreements from, say, January 2021. QuickBooks uses the summary journal entries to build the monthly cash accounts for January 2021.

- Empties the audit trail: QuickBooks keeps track of the people who filed certain transactions. The audit trail may have unexpected consequences if QuickBooks files are reorganized. You may delete the audit trail before to the "removed closed transactions on or before" date by cleaning up a business file and telling QuickBooks to compress it. In other words, when QuickBooks removes old, paused transactions, the audit trail for those transactions is also eliminated.

Generally speaking, you should make a copy of the QuickBooks data file and set it away before condensing a file. The operational business file's size is then decreased. However, the same phrase that causes a QuickBooks business file to decrease may also result in one that is almost empty. Most people seldom ever require this option. The only QuickBooks users I can think of who would want to produce almost empty company files are certified public accountants and financial advisers, who are able to create business data files with the majority of the lists pre-populated. These files may be shared with other departments or customers once they have been used. You should know that the archive command exists, but I won't bother you with the details of how to use it to create an almost empty business file.

Basics of cleanup

The process is much easier if you know the ins and outs of storage. The following are the steps to compress the QuickBooks business file:

- **Select File > Condense Data under Utilities:** QuickBooks displays the "Condense Your Company File" dialog box.
- Click Next after selecting the radio option labeled "Remove the Transactions You Select from Your Company File." The "Condense Data" dialogue box opens.

+ **Click the option box labeled "Transactions before a Specific Date."** This option is seen in the picture below. It tells QuickBooks to make a backup copy of the QuickBooks data file and shrink the size of the current business file. You might have eliminated transactions in Step 2. The working copy of the firm data file would then be smaller as a result of QuickBooks eliminating these outdated, paused transactions.

+ **Indicate the date on which transactions should be removed.** You may determine when halted deals should be deleted by entering a date in the date field if you wish to thin up your QuickBooks file by eliminating transactions that occurred on or before December 31, 2020. In the event that your QuickBooks business file becomes too large, feel free to delete just halted deals. You may deal with a 25MB, 50MB, or even 100MB (megabytes) QuickBooks corporate file with ease. It is standard procedure to eliminate outdated, closed transactions from a QuickBooks file in order to "condense" it. But you can also use the "Condense" command to create files with just a certain range of transactions or without any transactions at all. For instance, you may choose the "All Transactions" option choice to produce a file that contains just lists and preferences and no transactions.
+ **After you have finished defining which transactions QuickBooks should delete, click Next.:** QuickBooks displays a "Condense Data" dialog box.
+ **Indicate the format for the transaction summary:** A popup titled "Condense Data" will appear when you wish to see previous transactions in QuickBooks, asking you how you would want the data to be condensed. One summary journal entry, monthly summary entries, or no summary at all are your options. Simply choose the radio option that matches your desired summary approach to make your

selection. (The second option—having QuickBooks create monthly summary entries—is what most users use to create comparison reports.)

⬥ **After you have finished defining how QuickBooks should summarize transactions, click Next:** QuickBooks shows the third Condense Data text box, as you can see.

⬥ **Click Next after selecting the reduced inventory transaction method:** If you have old inventory transactions in your file, you may instruct QuickBooks to delete them when you see the fourth Condense Data box. Select the "Summarize Inventory Transactions (Recommended)" radio option to avoid this. Click the "Keep Inventory Transaction Details" radio choice if you would want to save previous transaction details. The fourth Condense Data text box (not shown) will ask you which transactions should be regarded as finalized once you click Next.

⬥ **Click Next after selecting which transactions need to be deleted:** By ticking boxes, you may indicate which transactions should be removed prior to the removal date. Regardless of whether these transactions are uncleared, tagged as To Be Sent, To Be Printed, etc., they will be erased. For QuickBooks to completely comprehend what an old or halted transaction that has to be erased is, further information is needed. Click "Next." before you get to the fifth Condense Data box.

⬥ **Click Next after selecting any necessary list cleaning:** In the fifth Condense Data box, you may instruct QuickBooks to purge some of the lists and eliminate outdated, halted transactions in order to reduce the size of the business file and make it simpler to deal with. Additionally, you may check the boxes instructing QuickBooks to delete unused accounts, users, suppliers, and other items. In QuickBooks, a sixth text box named Condense Data shows up when you click Next. This window notifies you that QuickBooks will start the archiving process by

114

making a copy of the file, which might take anywhere from a few minutes to many hours.

+ **Select "Start Condense."** QuickBooks begins the process of compressing the data file.
+ **When asked, create a backup of the data file.** QuickBooks will ask you to backup the QuickBooks business file before steaming starts, which is the same as preparing the file for steaming during a compressed operation or at any other time. QuickBooks will make a duplicate of your business file for later use after you have backed it up. The working copy of the file will be cleaned up in accordance with your directions. Remember that if your file is really huge, the cleaning process may take hours.

A few methods for cleaning and archiving

It's usually easy to figure out when and how to clear up or remove your QuickBooks business file. Before deciding to reduce the file size, make sure QuickBooks is still operating efficiently, that lists with extraneous items don't bother you too much, and that the data file hasn't gotten out of hand (around 1GB). Cleaning up won't assist you in many situations; in these situations, you can still obtain comprehensive and thorough financial information. The following is what my technical editor has asked me to do: Clean up the file first. Second, if you require a smaller QuickBooks file, save it and load it again. This is due to the possibility that not all data will always be deleted when a cleaning procedure is done. At the end of the year, once you or your CPA have made any last-minute changes, you should also make a backup copy of the QuickBooks data file.

This will assist you in clearing your QuickBooks and getting rid of old files. Archiving the QuickBooks data file is another smart idea. Making an archival duplicate of the data file is a smart idea if you use QuickBooks to compile your financial statements or tax return. In this manner, if you need to explain a figure in those papers, you can always consult the archival copy of the data file. Someone else may not be able to explain a figure on a tax return or financial statement if you see the QuickBooks data file after they have made a modification. One of the problems I raise with QuickBooks is that users have the ability to purposefully or unintentionally change past transactions. This suggests that if a transaction from a previous year that was used to determine your total revenue is changed, you cannot trust the numbers on your tax return or bank records that reflect that income. Doesn't this make perfect sense? You can always go back and look at which QuickBooks transactions are supporting a certain number if you have a backup of the QuickBooks data file, which is where you obtained the numbers for your financial statements and tax returns. It is advised that you consult a tax professional or certified public accountant (CPA) if you are still unclear about the possible repercussions of making changes to QuickBooks data used to create a financial statement or tax return after the documents have been made public.

CHAPTER FOURTEEN
UNDERSTANDING REGULATIONS AND COMPLIANCE

Knowing the requirements for compliance (such as the CCPA and GDPR)

In the current digital environment, managing financial data requires you to make sure that different data protection laws are followed. You must comprehend the needs of these rules, such as the California Consumer Privacy Act (CCPA) and the General Data Protection Regulation (GDPR), in order to preserve consumer information and uphold confidence. The details of these rules as they apply to QuickBooks users are covered in detail in this tutorial.

Regulation for General Data Protection (GDPR)

An overview of GDPR

The General Data Protection Regulation (GDPR), a data protection law in the European Union (EU) with the main objective of protecting the personal information of EU residents and guaranteeing their privacy rights, became mandatory for all companies, regardless of location, that process the personal data of EU residents on May 25, 2018.

Important GDPR Principles

- **Lawfulness, Fairness, and Transparency:** All relevant rules and regulations must be followed while processing data.
- **Purpose Limitation:** Information should only be gathered for clearly defined, legitimate purposes; it should not be used for purposes unrelated to those purposes.
- **Data Minimization:** The information gathered should be adequate, relevant, and restricted to that which is necessary for processing purposes.
- **Accuracy:** People's personal data must be accurate and, if changed, maintained up to date.
- **Storage Limitation:** Personal data should only be kept in a manner that enables data subjects to be identified for as long as absolutely required.

- ♣ **Integrity and Confidentiality:** It is crucial to process personal data safely. This covers protections against accidental loss, destruction, or damage in addition to illegal or unauthorized access.

Individuals' Rights under GDPR

- ♣ **Right to Access:** First, it is a basic human right to have access to one's data and information about how it is processed.
- ♣ **Right to Rectification:** This provision enables people to seek the correction of inaccurate personal information.
- ♣ **Right to Erasure:** Enables individuals to request that their personal data be deleted.
- ♣ **Right to Restrict Processing:** People have the "Right to Restrict Processing" to request that certain uses of personal data be limited.
- ♣ **Right to Data Portability:** This allows users to request that their data be moved to a different controller in a format that is widely used and machine-readable.
- ♣ **Right to Object:** People may object to the processing of personal data in certain circumstances.

GDPR Compliance and QuickBooks

QuickBooks users must take a number of steps to guarantee GDPR compliance:

- ♣ **Data Mapping:** Make a data map that displays all of the personal data you collect, along with the places where it is stored and the procedures used to process it in QuickBooks.
- ♣ **Permission Management:** Ensure that you obtain the express permission of EU customers before collecting and processing their data.
- ♣ **Data Security:** To protect sensitive data stored in QuickBooks, enforce strict security procedures.
- ♣ **Access restrictions:** Establish access restrictions to ensure that personally identifiable information may only be seen by authorized individuals.
- ♣ **Data Subject Requests:** Create protocols for handling requests from data subjects, such as those for access, deletion, or correction of personal data.
- ♣ **Data Breach Notification:** The sixth phase in the data breach notification process is to set up procedures for identifying, disclosing, and looking into data breaches.

The CCPA, or California Consumer Privacy Act,

An overview of the CCPA

The California Consumer Privacy Act (CCPA), a state law that went into effect on January 1, 2020, to improve consumer protection and privacy rights for Californians, applies to companies that gather personal information from California residents, meet certain requirements, and are for-profit.

Essential CCPA Principles

- **Transparency:** Companies must be upfront about the kinds of personal information they collect and the rationale behind it.
- **Control:** Consumers are entitled to know what information is collected about them, who receive it, and how to prevent data sales.
- **Accountability:** Businesses must make sure that the right security measures are in place to protect the private data of their clients.

Individual Rights under the CCPA

- **Right to Know:** Clients are entitled to know what types of personal data a business has collected about them, as well as how to access and update this data.
- **Right to Delete:** Under some circumstances, customers may request that their data be deleted.
- **Right to Opt-Out:** Customers have the option to refuse to have their personal data sold.
- **Right to Non-Discrimination:** If customers use their CCPA rights, they are entitled to a discrimination-free workplace.

CCPA Compliance and QuickBooks

In order to use QuickBooks in a fashion that conforms to the CCPA, you must:
- **Data Inventory:** To begin, collect as much personal data as you can from Californians. Then, use QuickBooks to see how everything fits together.
- **Updates to the Privacy Policy:** The CCPA requires privacy policies to be updated with disclosures about the kinds of personal information acquired, where it is obtained, and why it is being collected.
- **Management of Consumer Rights:** Install mechanisms to handle consumer requests for access, deletion, and opt-out.

- **Opt-Out Mechanisms:** Ensure that clients may quickly learn how to avoid having their private data sold to other parties.
- **Data Security:** To stop breaches and illegal access to personal data, bolster data security protocols.

QuickBooks Compliance Implementation

Top Techniques for CCPA and GDPR Compliance

- **Regular Audits:** You should regularly audit your data collection, processing, and storage procedures to ensure compliance with CCPA and GDPR regulations.
- **Training and Awareness:** Employees need to get instruction on data privacy regulations and their roles in ensuring that the business complies with them.
- **Data Minimization:** Only acquire the information needed for your company and refrain from gathering extraneous personal data.
- **Third-Party Management:** Keep an eye on any outside providers' procedures to ensure they abide with the California Consumer Privacy Act and the General Data Protection Regulation.
- **Incident Response Plan:** Make sure you test and have an incident response plan in place for when a data breach occurs.

Features of QuickBooks to Promote Compliance

- **User Permissions:** QuickBooks' permissions settings make it simple to control who may access what personal data.
- **Audit Logs:** Use QuickBooks' audit log feature to keep track of who made modifications to financial data and what they did.
- **Data Encryption:** Make sure that any data sent and stored via QuickBooks is encrypted to guard against unauthorized access.
- **Frequent Updates:** Keep QuickBooks up to speed with the newest compliance features and security patches.

Making sure QuickBooks complies with industry norms

Among the most crucial considerations for ensuring that QuickBooks complies with industry requirements are the legal environment, data security, accounting best practices, and staying current with technological advancements. **We've provided a thorough guide below to ensure QuickBooks is meeting market standards.**

Adherence to Regulations

Comprehending Industry Regulations

Every economic sector has its own set of rules and laws. Knowing which regulations apply to your industry is crucial, whether they are International Financial Reporting Standards (IFRS) globally or Generally Accepted Accounting Principles (GAAP) in the US.

Frequent upgrades and updates

The company that makes QuickBooks, Intuit, often releases updates to improve the program's usefulness and comply with regulatory changes. Make sure you are using the most current version of QuickBooks and enable automatic upgrades to stay in compliance with the most recent requirements.

Adapting QuickBooks to Industry-Specific Requirements

Versions of QuickBooks tailored to the retail, manufacturing, non-profit, and other industries are available. With the unique features and reports in these versions, you may continue to adhere to industry-specific requirements.

Security of Data

Establishing Robust Access Controls

Ensure that QuickBooks is only accessible by those who are authorized. Use role-based access controls to ensure that employees may only access the information they need to perform their duties.

Frequent backups

Make frequent backups of your QuickBooks data to prevent loss. Use cloud storage or both on-site and off-site backup solutions to ensure that data can be recovered in the case of cyberattacks or hardware failure.

Secure Connections with Encryption

Verify that data communications are encrypted in QuickBooks and other systems. Use secure connections (SSL/TLS) while sending data and encrypt stored data to protect critical financial information.

Accounting Best Practices

Precise Documentation

Verify that QuickBooks records are up to date and accurate. Regularly reconcile accounts and appropriately categorize transactions to keep correct financial records.

Frequent Evaluations and Audits

You should audit and check your QuickBooks data often to ensure that it is correct and up to date. This might be helpful in identifying discrepancies or potential issues before they become more serious.

Education and Training

Ensure that all users of QuickBooks have been adequately trained on both the product and the relevant accounting principles. Maintaining efficiency and compliance requires staying up to date with new features and improvements.

Combining Different Systems

Smooth Integration

Verify if QuickBooks integrates well with the other software used by your business, such as inventory management, payroll, and customer relationship management. This reduces the possibility of errors and helps maintain consistency in the data.

Utilizing APIs

Use the APIs to integrate and automate QuickBooks. This might lead to enhanced functionality and smooth data flow between QuickBooks and other company platforms.

Keeping abreast on technological developments

Cloud-Based Computing

QuickBooks Online is more flexible and user-friendly than ever before due to its cloud-based architecture. Cloud solutions often perform better than their desktop application equivalents in two areas: security and compliance.

Access on the Go

Use the QuickBooks mobile apps anytime you need to view your financial information. Always abide by your organization's data security policy while accessing QuickBooks on a mobile device.

AI and automation

Utilize QuickBooks' AI and automation features more effectively to reduce errors, streamline tedious tasks, and boost output.

Industry-Specific Functionalities and Personalization

Dashboards and Reports

Use the customizable reports and dashboards in QuickBooks for measuring KPIs particular to your industry. This facilitates making educated decisions and adhering to industry norms.

Modules with specialized functions

Utilize modules and add-ons that are specific to your industry. Among the services that QuickBooks offers that are specialized to a certain industry are payroll, inventory, and project management.

External Certifications and Audits

Audits by Third Parties

Make sure an independent party audits your QuickBooks setup and financial records on a regular basis. This provides an unbiased assessment of compliance and possible trouble spots.

Accreditations

To demonstrate that your business complies with industry standards, such as SOC 2 (Service Organization Control) for data security, consider obtaining certification. Obtaining these certifications might assist you win over your customers' and other stakeholders' trust and confidence.

Records and Guidelines

Extensive Records

Keep thorough records of every configuration parameter, user permission, and integration point associated with your QuickBooks installation. This documentation is essential for audits, troubleshooting, and continuity checks.

Rules and Guidelines

Establish and enforce policies and guidelines pertaining to QuickBooks use. This includes data entry methods, backup procedures, and guidelines for handling private financial information.

Taking responsible care of sensitive data

The QuickBooks file is one of the most important components of any business. Use the advice in this article to safeguard it against fraud and intrusions. In the current digital era, you need take additional care to protect sensitive data, especially that which is necessary for managing your company. The last thing you need is for your accounting data to be compromised or stolen. It would be much worse if your data breach caused your clients or consumers to experience the same problem. There are several ways to protect oneself from threats both within and outside the body. By combining common sense, strict standards, and QuickBooks' built-in safeguards, you can prevent data loss or theft for your business. Here are some steps you may take to protect the data of your business.

Protect Your Systems

Updating your operating system may seem like common sense, but it's also one of the best ways to protect your data. To safeguard all of your computer's applications and data, use security software from a reliable antivirus and malware provider. Use two-factor authentication wherever you can, create strong passwords using a password generator, and keep all of this information in a secure place. Additionally, QuickBooks Desktop will remind you to change your password every ninety days. Although it may frustrate you, this is an essential security measure for your data.

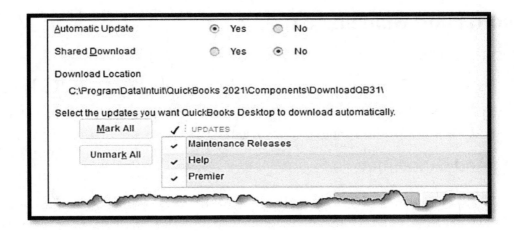

Backups and Updates

Keeping QuickBooks up to date is also very important. Although we recommend automating updates, you have the option to initiate them manually. From the Help menu, choose Update QuickBooks Desktop. You can use this tool by selecting the Options tab. Regular backups that are safely stored are essential to data security overall. According to the IT proverb, "Two is one and one is none," meaning that if you just have one copy, you won't have a backup in case of a breakdown. In the event that an attacker compromises your system, it is crucial to have the ability to restore your most recent QuickBooks file while your system is secure. Go to File | Back Up Company to create a backup, either locally or online. Use one of these tools to end the day after entering data into QuickBooks each day. If you don't know how to do it, we can help you with disaster recovery.

Smartphones and Networks

Maintaining the integrity of your network infrastructure is also essential since a breach at one workstation might affect all of your linked PCs. **Here's what I can do to help:**

- Tightly forbidding employees from installing unauthorized software and doing pointless internet browsing.
- Educating employees on proper email handling practices, such as avoiding opening attachments from unfamiliar senders, checking emails during business hours, confirming the sender's address, carefully reviewing links before clicking, etc.
- You may use a pay-as-you-go managed IT service or install software to keep an eye on your network.

Do your staff have access to mobile phones via the company? Verify if their safety measures are adequate. Establish measures to safeguard them. Instruct your team to desist from installing personal programs or utilizing them on public Wi-Fi networks at all costs.

Possible Internal Fraud

It is never imagined by any company owner that their workforce will commit theft. The financial repercussions may be considerable, however, and it does occur. Restricting staff access to vital information in QuickBooks Desktop may help lessen the probability of becoming a victim.

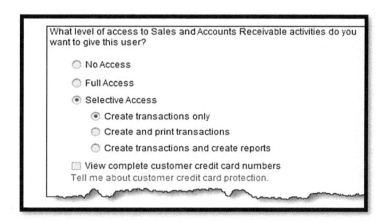

If you want to set up users, go to Company and then click on Set up Users and Passwords. You must be identified as the Admin. Give an account login and password by clicking the "Add User" button. Get in contact with us if you have any queries regarding the quantity of individuals your license can manage or if you need to add more. After that, choose QuickBooks from the list of options and click the button next to Selected Regions. Click Next again. You may give this user access to certain areas, like Purchases, Accounts Payable, and Checking and Credit Cards, on the following pages. When the wizard is nearly complete, click Finish. A background check may also be required when hiring someone who will have access to QuickBooks. It's becoming more and more commonplace for businesses. QuickBooks provides additional features to help with the investigation of suspicious activity. For example, the Audit Trail may be accessed under Reports | Accountant & Taxes | Audit Trail. This report includes information on every transaction that has been added or changed. Additional helpful reports to keep on hand are Missing Checks, Voided/Deleted Transactions, and Vendor Purchases. By routinely reviewing these reports, you can quickly detect internal fraud and lessen its effects.

A Never-Ending Practice

When you're busy operating your company every day, it's easy to lose sight of the necessity to keep your QuickBooks data (and all of your computer's hardware and software) safe. Cybercriminals depend on you to assume that your business isn't important enough to deserve their attention, which is why you could be as susceptible as a huge organization. Even if criminals don't manage to take your money, they may nevertheless inflict irreversible damage to your data, which can deplete your resources quicker than you would expect. Always be alert, follow best practices, and create a regular security check plan to lessen vulnerability. Always keep security in mind while dealing with money, but particularly when doing it online. Please let us know if we can help you set up procedures and safeguards for your company. We are available to assist you with any questions you may have about QuickBooks or its operation.

Security First in Cloud-Based Accounting

Security's Significance in Cloud Accounting

There has never been a more important moment for companies to adopt a "cloud first" approach, which transforms financial management by offering unparalleled convenience, efficiency, and accessibility. With every new cloud instance, however, a security storm might be building.

- In 82% of situations, data stored on the cloud was compromised. IBM report
- Eighty percent of businesses had at least one cloud security incident in the previous year. The Snyk report

The most significant security concerns and obstacles to cloud adoption are threats and hacks. Although QuickBooks Online's robust features satisfy the dynamic needs of modern businesses, the platform's cloud hosting does present significant security risks. However, if you take steps to safeguard QuickBooks Cloud Accounting, you may create a secure cloud environment that will preserve your clients' private financial data and gain their trust.

Recognizing Possible Hazards in QuickBooks Cloud Settings

Uncontrolled Surface of Attack

The entire number of possible access or extraction points that an unauthorized user may try is known as the attack surface. With all the interfaces, APIs, and user access points in cloud systems, this surface may become rather big.

For instance, a business that uses QuickBooks Cloud Hosting but neglects to put in place sufficient security measures may suffer severe repercussions. Once hackers get access to these interfaces, they may be able to take advantage of vulnerabilities to steal private financial information.

Solution: To reduce attack surfaces, security measures should be routinely reviewed and updated.

Human Error

Human error is one of the main causes of security breaches. Examples of human mistake include using weak passwords, accidentally exchanging data, and handling sensitive data improperly.

For instance, if staff members exchanged an email with their QuickBooks Cloud Hosting login information with a phishing scammer or stored the password on their computer, the company's financial information may be exposed.

Teaching employees to recognize and avoid phishing and related tactics is the solution.

Inaccurate setup

It occurs when cloud settings' security weaknesses are not sufficiently fixed. It could occur when updates or modifications are being made during the installation process.

Example: If QuickBooks Cloud Hosting user access control is not properly implemented and unauthorized individuals gain access, financial or sensitive data may unintentionally be made public online.

The solution is to periodically review and ensure that the QuickBooks Cloud Hosting settings are set up correctly.

Breach of Data

When sensitive information is accessed and recovered without authorization, it can lead to a data breach, which can cause financial loss, damage to one's reputation, and legal repercussions.

Example: If a cyberattack were to succeed or hackers were able to access the QuickBooks Cloud Hosting service due to insufficient security requirements, financial records, payroll data, and customer information might be stolen.

Solution: The answer is to utilize QuickBooks' built-in security features, such data encryption and multi-factor authentication, to protect critical data.

Understanding Other Threats in the QuickBooks Cloud Settings

The Zero-Day Exploits

A software vulnerability that has not yet been patched because the vendor is not aware of it is known as a zero-day exploit. These vulnerabilities can be exploited by attackers before developers have a chance to fix them.

For instance, malicious actors might discover an unpatched weakness in QuickBooks Cloud's authentication system and utilize it to gain unauthorized access to user accounts. Data theft may occur prior to the QuickBooks developer Intuit deploying a patch.

Solution: In order for QuickBooks to withstand recently discovered vulnerabilities, it is necessary to keep it updated with all of Intuit's security patches and upgrades.

APTs, or advanced persistent threats

Cyberattacks known as advanced persistent threats (APTs) infiltrate a network covertly and remain undetected for an extended period of time.

An example of a targeted APT attack would be one that targets a specific company that uses QuickBooks Cloud. The hacker enters the network through a phishing email and, over the course of several months, steals confidential financial data without anyone noticing. This compromises critical data and results in a significant financial loss.

Solution: It is advised to employ sophisticated monitoring tools and threat detection systems in order to promptly identify and respond to suspicious activity.

Insider Dangers

Insider threats occur when members of an organization misuse their access to confidential data for negative purposes.

For instance, a worker who has illegal access to QuickBooks Cloud may purposefully give away private financial data or sell customer information to competitors or online criminals. These threats present a special and difficult challenge since they target authorized system users who are trusted personnel.

Solution: It is advised to impose rigorous access limits and keep a careful eye on user behavior in order to identify and stop internal data exploitation and unauthorized access.

The Cyberattacks

Hacking, phishing, ransomware, and denial-of-service (DoS) assaults are merely a few examples of the numerous damaging activities that lie under the umbrella phrase "general cyberattacks."

For instance: Consider QuickBooks Cloud as an illustration. It could be compromised by ransomware, encrypting the company's financial information and preventing access until the ransom is paid. On the other side, QuickBooks may be the target of a denial-of-service attack that cripples the service and leaves users unable to access their financial data—especially during tax season.

Solution: The method is to defend oneself against assaults like ransomware and denial-of-service attacks by deploying a full cybersecurity solution. This solution should incorporate next-gen firewalls, antivirus software, and rolling data backups. Ace Cloud, like other respectable cloud hosting businesses, utilizes comparable security safeguards.

The Best Ways to Boost the Security of QuickBooks Cloud Accounting

To make your cloud accounting more secure, consider the following:

Robust Access Controls and Authentication

Enabling multi-factor authentication (MFA) is a robust security measure you may use to safeguard your cloud accounting systems. This will help prevent unauthorized access and limit user rights based on their roles and responsibilities.

Encryption of Data

Advanced Encryption Standards (AES) can be used to encrypt data while it is in transit and when it is being stored. By doing this, data is protected from illegal access or interception. It could be a crucial component of data security.

Regular security audits and vulnerability assessments

Finding faults with your cloud accounting system is simpler with frequent security audits and vulnerability assessments. Security specialists can help you discover issues and give solutions that will enhance operations.

Employee Awareness and Training Initiatives

Most safety problems are caused by human blunders. Staff staff should be trained on security best practices, frauds, risks, and dangers via training programs. It will aid you in training and teaching workers to be attentive against cyberattacks and keep themselves informed.

Strategies for Data Recovery and Backup

Organizations should have thorough data backup and recovery procedures in place to prevent data loss. If backups are carried out on a regular basis or for a predetermined amount of time, data may be recovered in the case of a cyberattack or accidental deletion.

Compliance with the Rules

Compliance with relevant regulatory regulations is essential to the legality and integrity of cloud accounting systems. Businesses must collaborate with compliance and legal experts in order to understand industry-specific regulations and create policies that meet these standards.

Continuous Vigilance and Threat Recognition

Providers should have ongoing monitoring and threat detection systems in order to quickly discover and address security issues. If we take the initiative, we can prevent little issues from turning into large disasters.

Guidelines for Open Security

Gaining customers' confidence requires having transparent security policies and procedures. Providers must be open and honest about their safety protocols, incident response strategies, and regulatory compliance. With this knowledge, you may confidently choose cloud accounting solutions.

Typical Risks to QuickBooks Accounting Security and How the Cloud Guards

The traditional method of setting up QuickBooks has limitations, despite the fact that its core features have evolved along with the times. QuickBooks may not have the most recent security features required to provide defense against the most recent cyberattacks if you install it locally on your desktop. This makes using QuickBooks potentially risky because it makes your data publicly accessible.

The Malware and Viruses

Is the notorious WannaCry malware attack from 2017 still fresh in your mind? It infected thousands of computers worldwide. Damages of over four billion dollars were sustained in 150 countries. Globally, viruses and malware represent a serious threat to the integrity of the system. Ransomware is one kind of harmful software that encrypts user data and then demands money to unlock it. Other infections, like Zeus, target the targeted people's financial accounts in order to do illegal activities. To properly defend oneself, one must be ready with modern solutions, even if a number of state-of-the-art antivirus programs have been developed to combat the growing ubiquity of these dangers. Consequently, now is the moment when companies who continue to use the traditional QuickBooks setup may be at serious danger. The great majority of businesses still use outdated terrestrial data networks with no modern substitutes. Malware attacks may easily target them, leading to a substantial loss of data that is necessary for the application. However, you can be confident that your company will have access to reliable security measures and that your data will be effectively safeguarded when you migrate your QuickBooks to the cloud. The cloud is periodically inspected by qualified experts and is equipped with the newest antivirus and antimalware software to fend off any kind of cybercrime. In order to protect your data from any cyberattacks, trustworthy service providers also use artificial intelligence methods to fix system flaws.

Unauthorized System Access

To say that the Internet is the hub of the modern world would not be an exaggeration. However, this has also allowed unauthorized others to access your information. For instance, visiting a website or doing out another apparently unimportant task might lead to illegal access to your QuickBooks, which could then reveal confidential information. Without the use of modern technology, the Internet offers a convenient way to access your

QuickBooks account, and this may occur without your consent. in the other hand, when you host QuickBooks in the cloud, it gives a full response to all of your issues about access. A solid firewall and Intrusion Detection and Prevention Systems (IDPS) are employed by the hosting provider to secure the vital data that you have stored on their servers. A firewall is a device that actively scans the data entering and leaving a computer connected to the internet. It filters out IP addresses that seem suspicious and prevents unwanted access. In a similar vein, an Intrusion and Detection Prevention System (IDPS) helps alert the network to any attempted attacks.

Unauthorized Access by Personnel

According to a study, an insider was in charge of about 77% of the data leaks that happened in the previous year. There are several ways that data can be unlawfully leaked, such as when an employee intentionally discloses data or when security protocols are unintentionally broken. Employees actively participating in the process, however, are responsible for the great majority of data breaches. For an accounting firm, dealing with this could be quite difficult. Accounting firms are in charge of managing private financial data, like bank statements, credit card numbers, and personal login passwords; if they don't protect this data, your customers may be in serious trouble. Furthermore, this might damage your company's image in the public eye and harm its reputation. By moving your QuickBooks to the cloud, you give yourself the option to limit administrative access and protect business data from staff members who could otherwise access it without authorization. You may limit data accessibility appropriately since everyone must have proper permission in order to utilize QuickBooks in the cloud. It allows you to track the activities of those positions and assess how easily accessible your QuickBooks data is based on the role you play in the company. By doing this, you might steer clear of what 41% of US businesses do, which is to provide unauthorized access to private information. Since all of the data stored on the cloud is stored on distant data servers, you won't suffer any major data loss in the event that your local data disks are stolen.

CHAPTER FIFTEEN
ABOUT QUICKBOOK INTEGRATION WITH OTHER TOOLS

Add-ons & Apps from Third Parties

Small company owners who are looking for the best accounting software will often find that QuickBooks Pro and QuickBooks Online score first on most websites. Additionally, this method is often used by accountants and certified public accountants. This made it possible for a large number of businesses to adopt it as their primary accounting software version. They could find it hard to abandon software they've been using for a long time, especially if their company grows or they need capabilities that QuickBooks doesn't provide. Because they are relevant to the job you perform, QuickBooks, which is more of a product that is not sector-specific, may not offer all of the features you need. Examples of this include things like advanced manufacturing management, inventory control, and time tracking. Fortunately, there are hundreds of QuickBooks add-ons and software that may be used to customize your basic QuickBooks to be a more business-appropriate tool. A fraction of the price of buying industry-specific ERP software may be used to achieve this. All desktop versions of QuickBooks, including the business, professional, and enterprise editions, include the feature of inventory.

The Self-Employed (Freelancer) edition, Essentials, and Simple Start are the only QuickBooks versions that do not fit into this category. Furthermore, this is true for QuickBooks Plus and Advanced, two of the four online versions. So why is it that a small business has to search elsewhere for merchandise? This is a simple explanation for why the inventory that comes with most ordinary versions of QuickBooks could be a little limited. Fundamentally, the integrated inventory modules will be able to provide you with real-time information and updates, as well as let you know what is presently in stock and what is being ordered. However, if you want to grow your business, you will need to think about the possibilities of launching new products and finding new ways to market them. Using a specialist inventory management system that can connect to your QuickBooks, you can turn your basic inventory into a supply chain management tool that helps you save time, save expenses, budget, and forecast demand (purchasing and sales). This might assist you in transforming your basic inventory into a more extensive program. Inventory add-ons, such as products with expiration dates, color/size matrices, and seasonal inventory levels, often have complex specifications that QuickBooks's normal inventory module is unable to meet.

FishBowl Inventory is our choice for inventory

FishBowl Inventory, an automated solution that markets itself as a way to bridge the gaps in existing QuickBooks services, is available to QuickBooks users. It offers sophisticated manufacturing features in addition to barcode scanning and component tracking. These are a few of the significant features it offers. The solution's objective is to help companies "compete with the big boys" who either lack the funds to buy full-featured manufacturing and distribution software or who think their QuickBooks processes are too embedded to switch to integrated ERP software. One of the first third parties to get Intuit's Gold Developer accreditation was FishBowl. It remains one of the most often used options for manufacturing and storage facilities looking to grow their operations while keeping their preferred accounting program. The setup wizard that Fishbowl provides is one of the easiest ways to move your current inventory data because of their long history of integrating with QuickBooks. You will spend more time understanding the ins and outs of the solution and less time implementing it since the inventory software will automatically input customer, vendor, component, and quantity data.

In addition to QuickBooks, FishBowl may be integrated with a number of other options that can help you streamline and centralize your manufacturing and storage processes. Here are a few examples: FedEx, UPS, Shopify, eBay, Amazon, and several more. Manufacturers need a bill of materials to produce each product, which may include the components, sub-assemblies, and raw materials used in the manufacturing process. Additionally, they must be able to modify their inventory levels in accordance with production levels. Some versions of QuickBooks can be used to manage manufacturing processes, although doing so requires a high level of program knowledge and proficiency, and workarounds will unavoidably be needed. The extra work needed to maintain your software so that it works the way you want it to effectively offset any apparent gain, even while the cost savings from having only one application might be energizing. In spite of this, QuickBooks is currently unable to precisely calculate labor costs and factory overhead costs throughout the production process. Because of the vast array of apps accessible in their app store, QuickBooks may be utilized as standalone solutions or as temporary manufacturing ERP software. QuickBooks may be used as manufacturing ERP software by integrating these applications.

xTuple is our manufacturing preference

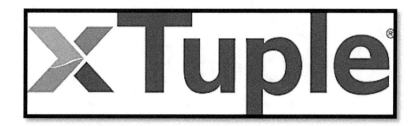

xTuple is an inventory management tool designed especially for growing enterprises. xTuple is helping companies that are centered on manufacturing and inventory to expand successfully with the help of management tools and industry best practices. Manufacturing software automates and integrates all of the tasks associated with production and back-office operations to form a single business system. Your company's efficiency could be greatly increased by xTuple solutions if it is in charge of taking sales orders, scheduling manufacturing, maintaining inventory shipping and receiving records, and making sure that all financial data is integrated. Your business may benefit from all of xTuple ERP's features, including manufacturing, planning, scheduling, inventory management, and MRP, by integrating xTuple with QuickBooks Desktop. No new accounting software has to be learned in order to do this. To put it simply, xTuple is a solution that fixes QuickBooks's flaws in the manufacturing sector, namely with regard to the distribution and planning of material needs management.

It is true that QuickBooks has time-tracking features that let your employees monitor how much time they spend on certain tasks. It is feasible to provide workers access that is limited to time entry only in order to keep them from accessing other areas of the system. Your business won't have to pay any more costs since this level of access doesn't count against the total number of QuickBooks licenses that are allowed. Companies that monitor time look for time-tracking software that will make it easier for them to manage payroll, create invoices (for the time that is chargeable), and automate calculations. Additionally, it may be used as a staff management tool, helping the business keep track of how much time employees, contractors, and suppliers are spending on certain activities. For many small businesses that are just starting out, this first level of time tracking is only useful for a short time. Perhaps they would like better ways to automate their company processes, create schedules, let staff members' clock in and out from a variety of devices, and even enable GPS capabilities. To manage these complex functions, an add-on will need to be implemented.

TSheets is our Preference for Time Tracking

In 2017, the cloud-based time and employee tracking system TSheets was acquired by the accounting software business QuickBooks. Because of this acquisition, TSheets is among the easiest time-tracking options to connect with your QuickBooks program. Additionally, Intuit would specifically recommend using it in combination with their flagship accounting program. Administrators and company owners have instant access to the hours that workers have worked. GPS tracking may also provide you with quick information on who is working and where they are located. This is a highly desired attribute when it comes to a mobile workforce. Moreover, TSheets provides features like task pricing, project tracking, geofencing, and online timesheets that are intended to enhance the data that QuickBooks already provides. It is easy to generate reports that show which customers are serviced each week, where employees like to spend the majority of their time, and the labor costs associated with a particular project. With a starting price of only $10 per user per month (in addition to a baseline fee of $30 per month), TSheets is among the most affordable time tracking options on the market.

Because the user fee only applies to administrative users and does not include workers who are just inputting hours, you may easily let employees enter their own time without worrying about a per-employee payment. Project-based businesses comprise a significant portion of small businesses worldwide and may be found in over a dozen various sectors, including consulting, accountancy, and construction. These businesses can better organize their projects, handle project-related spending, monitor project budgets, and generate estimates by using project management apps that work with QuickBooks. Project management is the most crucial component of managing a busy company in the construction sector. With the help of these tools, you can keep your budget within your means while cutting costs, raising revenue, and improving team communication. Furthermore, a significant portion of the workforce in the construction industry could be on a building site all the time without ever setting foot in the office. This mobile worker needs a sophisticated way to enter their hours worked, make purchase requests, and keep track of important project data. Even while QuickBooks can handle simple task costing on its own, it will fall far short when it comes to project management. You can turn your QuickBooks accounting program into a construction management tool that can manage everything from project management and accounting to bidding and vendor quotes with the aid of a few add-ons. This development is favorable.

Buildertrend is our preference for construction project management

Buildertrend is a construction project management software that may be used by commercial contractors, house builders, specialist contractors, and home remodelers. The program covers every facet of corporate operations, starting with the pre-sales phase and moving on to project management, financial management, and customer management. By integrating cost codes, converting change orders to invoices, converting purchase orders to bills, converting cost codes to items, and merging contacts, you may minimize duplicate input when connecting QuickBooks with Buildertrend. You will get access to all of these features. Information about clients and projects, suppliers, project-related bills and costs, bills against purchase orders, owner invoices, and authorized timesheets will all be stored by Buildertrend. QuickBooks will still manage client payments, process bill payments, and keep track of spending not included in Buildertrend. Buildertrend will, however, keep data independently. When QuickBooks and Buildertrend are combined, users may find that there is some overlap between the two programs. The ability to control employment expenses in both apps would be an illustration of this. As a result of the integration, you may enter the data in the application that you are most used to using, and it will immediately update and appropriately correlate to the other program. Businesses that use both Buildertrend and QuickBooks may do more precise job costing for all jobs by re-entering job-specific expenses that started in QuickBooks into Buildertrend budgets. When managers are out in the field, they may easily submit purchase orders and subcontractor invoices, which are subsequently sent to QuickBooks. By creating a purchase order and uploading it to QuickBooks, you may balance your bank transactions and remove the need for managers to add this information later. With material purchases, managers may also do things in this manner. After the accounting program has been properly connected, you will be able to move bills from unpaid Buildertrend expenses to QuickBooks. Once those bills have been fully paid in QuickBooks, the related expenses in Buildertrend will also be shown as paid. As a result, there will be fewer occurrences of duplicate entries.

The accounting program QuickBooks has a built-in billing feature that lets you create, organize, and send invoices to your customers. in order to guarantee timely payment. You may charge customers and send them invoices with this module, which also includes a "Pay Now" option. The capabilities, which include the ability to track when they are received, seen, and paid, provide your business an easy way to collect the money that is due to it. The ability to create expert invoices is also a feature of QuickBooks' regular packages. This allows you to change the font sizes and colors, add your company's logo, and make further adjustments. Additionally, you will be able to integrate with other office applications that you may use, including Google Calendar, which helps to automate the creation of recurring invoices and allows you to enter billable hours. Given that QuickBooks software can create periodic invoices, take online payments, and provide warnings for unpaid bills, why would a business consider investing in a billing add-on? In other words, the billing features that come with QuickBooks can be regarded as basic or inadequate to complete your needs. It would be wise to look into the possibilities of integrating your billing system if your business produces a lot of invoices or requires a lot of revisions.

Core BQE is Our Choice for Billing

BQE Core, a business management software program created by BQE Software, is a flexible and strong tool with many capabilities, such as project management, time and expenditure tracking, invoice generation, and even accounting duties. The solution was created mainly for businesses that provide professional services in order to help members of project teams collaborate more effectively. Your business will have access to a highly potent time billing, accounting, and financial management option thanks to the combination of BQE Core and QuickBooks Online. Even though BQE Core is a fully functional company management and accounting software choice at this time, they understand that many businesses will choose to stick with QuickBooks for their general accounting, online banking, or even payroll. Given that BQE Core provides a project-based accounting method (hierarchical structure), QuickBooks may still offer the client-based accounting structure that many businesses have been used to. QuickBooks is able to maintain this structure as a result. BQE Core adds a lot of capabilities that QuickBooks does not have in its basic version and provides a significant enhancement to the billing process. The application includes more than twenty basic invoice templates including invoices for hourly, fixed fee, unit cost, and percentage contract types. It also offers the ability to create unique invoice templates if needed. The billing option becomes a true one-stop shop for all of your billing needs due to its direct connection to both time and expenses. Price schedules are also included to ensure that your invoices are always correct. Other billing features include workflow approval, split billing, automatic billing, billing schedules, and repeated bills.

The intense scrutiny they face and the rising need of financial transparency are two things that all government contractors have in common. One of the objectives associated with the usage of accounting software is the ability to continue to adhere to the criteria of the Defense Contract Audit Agency (DCAA), the regulatory agency in charge of auditing government contracts. These methods have been tried and tested and have been shown to be successful, so you should have a greater chance of passing a DCAA audit and staying in compliance with the Federal Acquisition Regulations (FAR). Although the DCAA does not officially certify any software, the term "DCAA compliant" describes software vendors that organize their operations in a way that is more suited for compliance. Accordingly, any accounting software that passes the system audit is said to be functioning in accordance with the DCAA. However, there are software providers that focus only on working with government contractors. They may thus provide assistance in making sure the software complies with any recommendations made by the government. You will require a third-party solution to match your QuickBooks with the laws, which include consistent labor dollar allocation, policies and processes geared toward FAR compliance standards, appropriate time-keeping that is reported daily, and more.

Although QuickBooks Online could comply with the DCAA, you will need them to make sure your QuickBooks is in compliance.

GovCon Connect is Our Choice for a Government Contractor

GovCon Connect is designed to provide government contractors using QuickBooks Desktop or Online the tools they need to pass DCAA examinations. The application is more likely to pass the DCAA accounting system assessments if it is "DCAA compliant," as is the case with any other software that makes such a claim. Having helped hundreds of contractors pass their audits, GovCon has been one of the most well-liked options for government contractors since its establishment in 2004. The approach allows for more possibilities to be eligible for firm-fixed-price contracts, time-and-material contracts, cost-plus-fixed-fee contracts, and subcontract awards. In addition to the standard accounting features that QuickBooks already provides, GovCon Connect offers additional features like timesheets, an enhanced chart of accounts, job costing, labor distribution, CLINN/task reporting, indirect rate calculation, contract management, and budget and preliminary indirect rate development. Three versions of GovCon are available: a basic edition for people starting their own company, a business edition with a wealth of reporting options, and a premiere edition for those who must develop labor rates and corporate indirect pricing. There is no need to go further since QuickBooks provides payroll services on its own. There are many reasons why your firm may be doing this. QuickBooks can be used as accounting software; however it is not appropriate for use as a payroll application. If you find a payroll program that is easy to use, you may choose to integrate it with the accounting software that you already know and use. Regardless of the reason for your choice, QuickBooks has a large selection of payroll add-ons. Selecting the best payroll software to assist you save time and effort is a big issue when it comes to processing payroll. This is due to the fact that most small companies are aware that handling payroll alone takes a substantial amount of time.

OnPay is Our Selection for Payroll

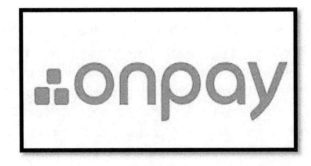

You may obtain full-service payroll with electronic tax filing and payments using OnPay and QuickBooks. It integrates human resource expertise and benefits that QuickBooks' payroll services do not in order to provide your employees the best service possible. Payroll tax calculations for all 50 states are also provided by OnPay, along with the ability to create W-2s and 1099s. You may choose from a variety of pay rates, unlimited monthly pay runs, and the ability to pay employees by direct deposit, debit card, or cheque. You can easily import employee-level data into QuickBooks, generate customized reports, and view your money anyway you like thanks to the software's smooth interface with QuickBooks. Additionally, QuickBooks allows you to create custom reports based on wage expenses monitored by location, class, pay type, or department.

CHAPTER SIXTEEN
DEBUGGING AND ASSISTANCE

Typical Problems and Their Fixes

Most of us have had some kind of issue while using QuickBooks. We have made every effort to provide a list of common QuickBooks issues and their solutions.

The Data Files Don't Update

The most current edition of QuickBooks may sometimes not be able to read the data record from the previous version while upgrading it version by version. Therefore, updating the information sheet is advised. You must stress everything before it occurs, which often occurs throughout the establishing interaction. To prevent any issues, be sure to do a confirmation on the information record before to removing the previous version or installing the updated version. To ensure you always have a fallback option, you should even provide the updated version alongside the previous one.

Failure to Restore Data Files

On occasion, upgrading verified data to a more recent version could be required. You will have to restore your data from an older version in such a scenario. It could be easy for a few of you. However, most of you would be reluctant to handle the file that has the financial details of your organization. In the event that you find yourself in this situation, here are several ways to restore your data files. Make an error-checked copy of the data file, and then restore it. This is the exact order that has to be followed. In the event that this rebuild is unsuccessful, confirm that the data file is on the local computer. According to QuickBooks, data files must be located on the C: drive. It suggests that even if the Q: drive is really on a shared local system, QuickBooks would handle your data file as if it were saved on a different disk. There could be an issue with QuickBooks' rebuild. Make a copy of the data file to the C:\ drive before rebuilding. You may move the data kingdom back to its original place after you've rebuilt it.

Terminate the Data File Connection

It is the most common issue and the most difficult to resolve. QuickBooks need to be more knowledgeable about the network connection of the data file. Even a little network problem might cause you to lose your connection. If you are certain that QuickBooks is setup properly, use the QuickBooks Connection Diagnostic Tool to determine the issue. Try turning off your antivirus program and then turning on the firewall again if it isn't blocking the connection.

When the Reinstallation Doesn't Work

If you ever need to reinstall QuickBooks, pay special attention to this. Before installing the latest version of QuickBooks, remove the old one. When you know what to anticipate, using Windows' built-in uninstaller to remove QuickBooks is simple. Proceed to remove the C:\Program Files\Intuit\QuickBooksXXX directory (release number XXX) and the C:\Windows\Users\Documents And Settings\Program Data\Intuit\QuickBooksXXX folders (release number XXX). To reduce frequent QuickBooks mistakes, make sure the data is backed up before making any changes.

QuickBooks Performs Slowly When Using Multiple Users

This one is difficult since a user may now run across several issues. Any kind of sluggishness is frequent. After ruling out hardware problems, users may have to deal with data file difficulties. In this case, clearing the cache on your computer is the simplest solution. There is one more way to speed up QuickBooks while using it in multi-user mode. There is always the option to turn off the Audit Trail. This is the action you need to do.

The QuickBooks client computer is unable to find the server's data file

If you use QuickBooks, you may have seen that the client computer sometimes has issues recognizing the server's data file. In each situation, we advise beginning by confirming that the server administration software is installed on the server's PC. If this doesn't work, you may try mapping the client system's disk to the server. Additionally, if the client can see the server, the Server Manager isn't working correctly.

Learn about the program for licensing

Let's say you need to find all of your documents. In such cases, you won't be able to see your license or product number! There is a remedy for every issue. You may look for them by pressing [F2] or [Ctrl]1 when QuickBooks launches and you are in your data file. (Unless you wrote that validation code down.) If you need to reinstall, you must re-register.

Documents won't print on the new printer

People often misunderstand this fundamental principle. When utilizing a new printer, always print documents. **That's how simple it is.**

```
• Close QuickBooks
• Search for the file qbprint.qbp
• Rename qbprint.qbp to qbprint.qbp.old
• Restart QuickBooks
• Start Printing your document
```

When an Administrator Password Is Lost

Could someone help you remember your QuickBooks administrator password? Rest assured that there is a way to retrieve forgotten passwords. Or maybe the password was not given to you by the previous administrator. You may quickly recover the password by using the QuickBooks Automated Password Reset Tool. Usually, this method works.

It is not possible to move or copy QuickBooks data files

Many of us often do the task of backing up our data. Have you tried transferring the QuickBooks file to another portable drive? That will show that the file is protected, so avoid doing so at all costs. Thankfully, a duplicate of your data file may be saved. After turning off QuickBooks, choose "Start" and then "Enter Services." Look for QuickBooks-related services. The file may be easily copied and pasted after the services have been turned off.

Ways to Reduce Issues Associated with QuickBooks

The history of QuickBooks must be taken into account. We can help if you're experiencing issues with QuickBooks. **These actions are necessary if you want your QuickBooks to operate as effectively as possible.**

- Once every seven days, review the paperwork for your business. Repair any damaged data as soon as you see it. QuickBooks' "Rebuild" tool is only helpful for manual data restorations, therefore users should be aware of it.
- Before using QuickBooks, always restart your PC.
- Close the QuickBooks window permanently just before you log out for the day.
- Close the QuickBooks window when not in use.

- If you are not actively using business data files, you should always log out of your account.
- At the conclusion of each day, shut down your computer and log out of the company's files.
- Switching to the single-user mode is advised if the data file is being utilized by only one person. QuickBooks may sometimes behave slowly while handling payroll-related tasks. Encourage other users to log off and do payroll-related tasks on their own.
- Avoid using zero lines when inputting QuickBooks transactions. You may wonder what more QuickBooks can do than handling your finances. These zero lines offer an additional target for data input, increasing the size of your file.
- Inaccurate information may sometimes be provided to people who create cash-based reports pertaining to inventories.
- Ensure that all printed or emailed forms are regularly cleared from the queue; do not allow a significant number of unprinted or emailed forms to accumulate.
- To avoid using up other people's resources, they should: Optimize reports; Send out bulk emails or print out statements before normal work hours, at night, at lunch, or at other off-peak periods.
- Running reports is a resource-intensive QuickBooks operation since it gathers a lot of data. Report printing and reporting optimization may save time and costs.

Fixing setup and installation issues

You may be trying to install QuickBooks as an update or as a first-time user, depending on your circumstances. Even the simplest QB installation may become rather difficult if even one part isn't working, no matter how hard you try. It's common for QuickBooks Desktop Installation Errors to occur, and when they do, users usually become quite upset and try to resolve the issue by restarting QuickBooks.

Typical Installation Mistakes

- **Error 1603:** This error appears when QuickBooks cannot start because it needs certain components, including the Microsoft.NET Framework, which may occur during installation.
- **Error 1935:** This error number indicates that there can be an issue with the Microsoft.NET Framework or any other third-party applications if it appears during installation.

- **System requirement errors:** A few minimal system requirements must be met for QuickBooks to install and function properly. If you don't follow these instructions, you run the chance of installation problems.

We must first identify the types of problems, their extent, and the specific strategies to use after we have identified them before we can start to resolve QuickBooks Desktop installation issues. We start with a summary of every issue that might occur while setting up QuickBooks.

QuickBooks Desktop Install Error Causes

Here, we'll examine the possible reasons for the QuickBooks Desktop Installation Errors in each of the listicle.

A. Because Windows OS lacks the most current updates, QuickBooks Desktop cannot be installed on it.

B. If you're using an outdated installation file, QuickBooks Desktop may not install properly.

C. It is likely that a corrupted prior installation of QuickBooks Desktop is interfering with the present installation.

D. Issues with your computer's hard drive may also be the source of trouble installing QuickBooks or other software.

E. One of the main causes of QuickBooks Desktop installation issues is Windows User Account Control Settings (UAC).

F. When the Windows Firewall places limitations on QuickBooks, the installation process may be halted and other issues may occur.

G. Other security programs, such antivirus or malware protection software, may be the source of QuickBooks installation errors.

These elements combine to produce QuickBooks Desktop Installation Errors, which may occur in a few distinct ways that we'll discuss later.

Easy Ways to Resolve QuickBooks Desktop Install Issues

In this post, we'll demonstrate how to resolve QuickBooks installation issues using time-tested solutions.

Solution A: Get the Latest Features and Bug Fixes by Updating Windows

Keeping Windows updated not only allows you to enjoy the newest features, but it also resolves problems with previous upgrades that might have caused problems installing QuickBooks.

- To begin, go from the Start menu to the Settings menu.
- Select Windows Update after navigating to the Update & Security section.
- You may utilize the Check for Updates option here to check whether Microsoft has made any updates available for your Windows operating system.
- Download the most recent updates for your computer.
- Launch the installation right away to see whether the QuickBooks desktop installation problems have been resolved.

Solution B: To fix the problems with the current installation, reinstall QuickBooks

These procedures must be followed if QuickBooks Desktop is already installed on your computer and you're trying to install an upgraded version. You might try uninstalling and then reinstalling QuickBooks if you're experiencing issues installing it on your desktop.

- Open the business file with all of your data to start utilizing this solution.
- Making a duplicate of your corporate file and storing it on a local hard drive is the next step.
- Open the Control Panel, and then choose Programs and Features.
- From the list of apps that appear on the screen, choose QuickBooks.
- Click the QuickBooks icon's "Uninstall" button.
- The next step is to add OLD to the title of every folder in the Intuit folder directory.
- Next, follow the steps to check whether you can successfully reinstall QuickBooks.

Solution C: Rearrange the Hard Drive's Data

Use these procedures to defragment your hard drive if it is full and includes installation-unsuitable pieces:

- To access the place where you want to install QuickBooks Desktop, use the right mouse button on the drive icon.
- Select Tools after pressing on Properties, and then select Disk Defragment.
- This will restructure your drive's contents such that similar files are arranged in a row.
- Click Analyze, then choose Defragment, and then follow the wizard's instructions.
- You should install QuickBooks Desktop now to see if it resolves the issue.

Solution D: Adjust the User Account Control (UAC) Configuration in Windows

Because the UAC Settings are set higher than necessary, they may cause you problems when you attempt to install or use certain programs or their capabilities. To resolve issues with QuickBooks installation, let's adjust the Windows UAC settings.

+ Click the Start button, and then choose User Accounts to open the Control Panel.
+ After choosing Change UAC Settings, click Continue.
+ Before clicking OK, choose "Never Notify" and then uncheck it.
+ After restarting, try beginning the QuickBooks installation procedure over if you're still having issues.

Solution E: While installing QB, turn off the Windows firewall program.

The firewall's job is to keep harmful software and other threats out of your computer. You may need to turn off options that flag the installation as dangerous if you want QuickBooks to install without any problems.

+ Press the Start key on your keyboard to open the Control Panel.
+ Select System and Security to open the Windows security panel. Select Windows Firewall from there.
+ Toggle Windows Firewall on and off by pressing the On/Off button.
+ Locate the Windows Firewall icon and click it.
+ After turning off the firewall, try installing QuickBooks once again. If that resolves the issue, put the firewall back on.

Solution F: Create a QuickBooks Firewall Port Exception

Try adding QuickBooks to the firewall's exceptions list in the firewall's settings if the issues persist after you've turned it on. The procedure of switching firewall ports may be automated by certain applications. **Here are the steps to follow if you choose to do it yourself:**

+ Click the Windows button, and then type "Firewall" into the search bar.
+ Press Enter to choose Windows Firewall.
+ Tap the Advanced Settings button, and then locate the Inbound Rules box and right-click on it.
+ Then, to start generating a new rule, choose Port and click Next.
+ After selecting the TCP option, connect the ports that match the QuickBooks version you're using.
+ Next, choose Allow the Connection by clicking Next.

- Click Next and choose every profile in the resulting window.
- Next, press the Next button. Creating a rule is the next step.
- You should label it something like "QBPorts(year)" for ease of use.
- Next, repeat steps 1 through 9 to build Outbound Rules, then click the Finish button.
- Restart your PC and open QuickBooks to see whether the issue has been resolved.

Solution G: Check your antivirus settings to see if they're interfering with the installation of QB

The first step is to find out whether QuickBooks installation is being blocked by your antivirus program. Before you can add QuickBooks to the secure zone in the settings, you must provide it the required access and permissions so that it can get over antivirus restrictions. It is advisable to contact the relevant support for that, since steps may vary from program to program.

Solution H: Use the QB Install Tool to Correct Typical QuickBooks Desktop Installation Issues

Intuit offers a number of ways to address any issues or errors that can occur while using QuickBooks. One such application that helps resolve installation issues is the QuickBooks Install Diagnostic Tool. This tool can swiftly install QuickBooks Desktop; here's how to start it after it's installed.

- The QuickBooks Install Diagnostic Tool cannot be used until QuickBooks Tool Hub has been installed.
- Install Intuit on your PC by visiting the official website.
- Launch the Tool Hub installation procedure, and when it is complete, launch it on your computer.
- From the Installation Issues section, choose QuickBooks Install Diagnostic Tool. This tool will immediately identify the contributing elements to
- Quickly resolve any installation issues.
- Try installing QuickBooks Desktop once again, and use the QB Install Diagnostic Tool to determine whether the issues have been resolved.

Other Solutions for Installation Issues with QuickBooks Desktop

If none of the above solutions work to fix the QuickBooks Desktop installation problems, try the following fixes:

- **Check Your Computer for Malware and Viruses:** You may never be sure when a malicious website may have allowed a virus to infect your machine. This virus has the ability to stop almost every system function.
- **Delete Any Superfluous Files from Your System:** Junk files, like ordinary files, take up a lot of computer space, and if you don't delete them, QuickBooks installation may encounter issues. If these files are deleted to provide space, the installation will go more easily.
- **Verify that your Windows drivers are current:** Your system drivers, especially the installation drivers, may have been worn down by the most recent Windows update. If this occurs, they may begin to misbehave and interfere with other computer applications. You must update and refresh your drivers in order to resolve this.
- **Fix Inaccurate Registry Entries for Windows:** A damaged registry inside your PC might be the source of issues. This problem may be resolved by using a registry repair program to fix the register.

You should immediately fix the.NET Framework if you are seeing the error notice "fix QuickBooks desktop install errors needs a net framework," so that QuickBooks may install without any issues. The.NET Framework is an essential part of Windows.

Final Thoughts

In this thorough guide, we have covered every aspect of using QuickBooks, from setting up a business file to managing regular transactions and generating important reports. QuickBooks is advanced tools that can help companies of any size meet their accounting needs. By following this guidebook, you may streamline your financial duties, reduce mistakes, and improve your understanding of the financial health of your business. Understanding QuickBooks will save you time and enable you to make better financial choices, whether you manage your own small business, oversee accounting for a company, or work as a freelancer. You must use and update QuickBooks often if you want to get the most out of it. You can be certain that QuickBooks will expand and change along with your business. Never cease researching its features, being informed about its current state, and looking for fresh approaches to improve your accounting practices. Thank you for completing this lesson. We hope that after reading this, you are ready to take advantage of QuickBooks and see your business grow.

INDEX

S